Paul Nesbit's

LONGS PEAK

Its Story and a Climbing Guide

Eleventh Edition
Revised and Updated by Stan Adamson

Grey Wolf Books, U.S.A.
Broomfield, Colorado

LIBRARY OF CONGRESS CONTROL NUMBER: 2005925727
ISBN:0-9768259-0-2 Paperback
Previous Editions: 1946, 1953, 1956, 1959, 1963,
                    1966, 1969, 1972, 1990, 1995

Printed on 60# Recycled paper
in the United States of America by:
Sheridan Books, Ann Arbor, MI
734.662.3291

PUBLISHED AND DISTRIBUTED BY
Grey Wolf Books, U.S.A.
4933 Grey Wolf Place
Broomfield, Colorado 80020
303-818-1876

Book Design, and Art Direction by:

A. J. Images, Inc.
Graphic & Communication Design
www.ajimagesinc.com — 303•696•9227
info@ajimagesinc.com

Front Cover Photo of Longs Peak East Face from Boulderfield.
—by Lloyd O. Timblin Jr.

Title page illustrations — by Paul Nesbit.

Although defeated again and again, mountains do not stay conquered. Man sallies forth upon them from comfortable havens in the valleys and retreats again for night or for the winter. When a climber stands upon the very tip of some great peak, he stands for only a moment of time, while the peak stands no less proudly on to be frequently surmounted, but never conquered. Neither need the spirit of man be conquered. He too can carry on in spite of temporary defeats; and may he always be eager for another climb or another try; indomitable, unconquerable.

Mountains are good for us; they get us to increase our efforts.

— Paul Nesbit

About the Author

Paul Nesbit first climbed Longs Peak in 1924, and was employed by Mrs. Enos Mills of the Longs Peak Inn during the summers 1925 through 1928 as a nature guide on Longs Peak. After that he continued to guide on Longs Peak from time to time. His last climb up Longs was as trip leader for the Colorado Mountain Club on August 1, 1965. He worked as Ranger Naturalist in Rocky Mountain National Park and Yosemite National Park, was owner and manager of Hewes-Kirkwood Inn at the foot of Longs Peak and was a teacher, photographer, and writer.

Paul Nesbit about 1940

He had a lifelong interest in the mountains, and spent much time studying nature, ecology and geology. Somewhat in the tradition of Enos A. Mills, he tried to get others into the mountains and to increase their interest in, and their enjoyment of them. He kept a written record of his trips for over 50 years, which covers more than 4,900 outings averaging over nine hours each. His records show 125 climbs up Longs Peak, of which 116 have been counted in the summit registers. He also climbed most of the mountains over 14,000 feet in Colorado.

Other books by the author include *Garden of Gods, Nez-Bits, New Techniques for Efficient Teaching* and *Instructive Nature Games.*

Norman Nesbit, Walter Tishma, Stan Adamson and Jim Detterline at Boulderfield on the day of Walter's 100th climb of Longs Peak.

Photo by — Brian Lewis

Introduction to the Eleventh Edition

The 11th edition of *Longs Peak: Its Story and a Climbing Guide* celebrates the 59th anniversary of the 1946 publication of Paul Nesbit's premier work on Longs Peak.

I have tried as much as possible to preserve Paul Nesbit's original, homespun style, which he developed over many years as a teacher, naturalist and guide; you can hear him speaking, as he would, on the trail, over the boulders, and up the Homestretch.

I have followed the convention of not using an apostrophe in the names of mountains, e.g. "Longs Peak."

In the several years since the 10th edition, this repository of Longs Peak lore has continued to attract a large readership. The new edition improves and updates the usefulness of this standard work in its field. Trails Illustrated's excellent topographical map on the back cover of the book provides a ready reference on the trail. Up-to-date statistical information was provided by Dr. Jim Detterline, National Park Service, Rocky Mountain National Park. Additional photographs from Lloyd O. Timblin, Jr., and Brian Lewis greatly enhance this edition. Additional proofreading and suggestions came from Pat Ament, Helen Hannen Donahue, Brian Lewis, Cleve McCarty, Dougald MacDonald and members of the editor's "Longs Peak Adventure" class conducted for five years for the Lifelong Learning program of the Boulder Valley Schools. Conversations with a number of the persons mentioned in the pages of this book during three historical symposia in connection with the Longs Peak Reunions in 1992, 1994 and 2001 also have brought improvements to the text. The continued assistance, support and encouragement of Norman Nesbit has been invaluable. Barbara Adamson assisted in text review for this edition. Karin Hoffman, creative director of A. J. Images, Inc. has greatly improved the readability of the text with a new layout and design of this edition's content.

The enduring significance of Longs Peak among the "fourteeners" of the Colorado Rockies has been enhanced by the information available in what everyone refers to as "The Nesbit book." We are pleased to offer this new edition of a proud tradition among the annals of climbing in Colorado, the "roof of the Rockies."

Stan Adamson
Broomfield, Colorado
May 2005

Paul Nesbit's FOREWORD to the Eighth Edition

In writing about Longs Peak, one has four general groups to keep in mind:
1. The large numbers of local residents and vacationists who are interested in reading about the mountain, and perhaps in having the personal experience of climbing it.
2. Those who, having climbed, become overly ambitious in comparison with their lack of experience and are tempted to dare climbs that are beyond their ability or at the wrong time of year.
3. The Rocky Mountain National Park Service officials who are concerned with the protection of the natural features and of everyone from the follies of the group in No. 2.
4. The expert, technical climbers who are practicing one of the world's greatest sports.

The aims, then, are to especially interest and encourage the first group, discourage the second, cooperate with the third, appreciate the fourth, and to provide information for all in the popular booklet which tells some of the things which most interested the 655 persons guided to the top by the writer, and the questions of numerous others.

This book was never intended to be a detailed work on the rather numerous technical climbing routes on Longs Peak. However, as an introduction to the world of rock engineering, we show nearly all known technical climbing routes on Longs Peak in various photographs and a table of these routes with an indication of their climbing difficulty. Those young tigers who are looking for more detailed climbing descriptions of these technical routes are encouraged to obtain a copy of *The High Peaks* by Richard DuMais. (See Bibliography for this and other titles by Briggs, Harlin, MacDonald and Roach).

An appreciation for kindly help and information is due many of the living persons named in the booklet. Some, who have passed on, were questioned by the writer beforehand. Wives and descendents of others have been helpful to supply information. Special credit is due to the late Warren Gorrell, Jr., who had gathered more information about Longs Peak than anyone else. Members of the National Park Service have been continuously helpful, Steve Hickman and David Butts for this edition in particular. David Rearick and Layton Kor have been particularly so regarding the Diamond climbs. Walter Fricke has compiled much information about technical climbs on Longs Peak and has been of much help in supplying information on these routes as well as many events of interest on the Peak. Suggestions or corrections are always welcome in order that each edition may be an improvement.

Tips and Suggestions
for a Successful Climb of Longs Peak

By Norman Nesbit

1. Good physical condition is most essential for a successful and enjoyable climb of Longs Peak. We suggest a hike up Twin Sisters mountain, and then a climb up Hallet Peak via the Flattop Mountain trail, would be good conditioning hikes for Longs Peak. If you live where there are no mountains nearby, you should be able to walk for twenty miles on the level in about seven hours and still feel you can do a few more miles if necessary.

2. Summer climbing season usually starts sometime in July, depending upon the amount of snow left over from the previous winter. Climbing season usually closes sometime in September, depending upon the first significant winter storm to hit the peak.

3. Hiking boots with rubber lug soles or good jogging or sturdy walking shoes should be used for this climb.

4. Items to take with you in your backpack for summer climbing include a warm jacket, light gloves, sunglasses, rain protection, small flashlight, water, first aid kit, camera, brimmed hat or cap, sunburn cream, and lunch with perhaps a sandwich, apple or orange, dried fruit, candy bar, and/or some of your favorite lunch items.

5. A very early start in the morning is strongly recommended to avoid common afternoon lightning storms, especially in July and August. A start up the trail by 3 to 4 a.m. is ideal, with a start after 5 a.m. not good unless you are in top physical condition for climbing.

6. It is the writer's experience that on the Longs Peak climb camping overnight several miles up the trail is not worth the extra effort of packing in your gear and setting up an overnight camp.

7. When starting out on the trail, make a conscious effort to walk more slowly than you feel inclined to do. A hallmark of older experienced climbers is their slow, deliberate pace, especially when first starting out. Also, when climbing above Boulderfield, avoid the inclination to take long steps from rock to rock. Taking shorter steps whenever possible is less tiring in the long run.

8. Water found in streams along the trail is no longer considered safe to drink. We recommend you take from one pint to one quart of water with you, and have a swallow or two from time to time along the trail.

9. Route finding should not be a problem on Longs Peak in the summer climbing season. There is a well-marked and used trail to Boulderfield, and on a good summer day several hundred people will probably be climbing on the Keyhole route. If you stay on this route you will be within sight of 30 to 50 or more people above and below you virtually all the time in the late morning and early afternoon.

10. If it takes you longer than five hours to hike from the Longs Peak Campground to the Keyhole, or ominous looking clouds are already gathering near the mountain when you get there, you should seriously consider turning around and giving the peak a try on another day.

11. When there is danger of lightning, you should stay off the summit and ridges and away from tall trees. Wait in a depression or bottom of a cliff. Usually the lightning storm will move on in 20-30 minutes.

12. The average round trip time for those in borderline to moderate condition will be 11 to 14 hours.

13. Typical weather around Longs Peak in July and August is clear or partly cloudy in the mornings, with scattered rain and lightning storms here and there all afternoon and often into the evening. Typical weather in September is significantly different, with a cloudless sky any time in the morning after sunrise assuring no rain or lightning until at least sunset. September can, and often does, bring the best climbing weather we have for the entire year. However, when bad weather does come, it can be a winter snowstorm, which can close the peak from further summer season climbing.

14. Although 4 and 5-year-old children have successfully climbed Longs Peak, we do not recommend children younger than 9 years old be taken on the climb.

15. If you get sick or light-headed from the effects of high altitude, try resting for 15-20 minutes, then start off very slowly and deliberately, taking short steps and breathing more frequently and deeply than you might otherwise feel necessary.

16. Horses are used by less than 1 percent of climbers these days, although in the 1920s, 30s and 40s about one third of all climbers rode horseback to Boulderfield.

17. There are 54 mountains in Colorado above 14,000 feet. At least half of them are easier to climb than Longs Peak, including Mt. Elbert, Colorado's highest mountain.

Stan Adamson's Longs Peak Adventure class at Granite Pass.

Photo by — Lloyd O. Timblin Jr.

Table of Contents

The sheer face of the Diamond, from Boulderfield.

Photo by — Lloyd O. Timblin Jr.

Longs Peak Described and Compared

In north-central Colorado, almost exactly half way between Canada and Mexico, lies one of the nation's best known mountain peaks. It enjoys an imposing position in the Front Range of the Rocky Mountains where it attracts the attention of great numbers of people who can see it from Denver and other nearby cities along the western edge of the Great Plains. In addition, Longs Peak is a central feature and the highest point in Rocky Mountain National Park. It thus dominates a rugged mountain area of unusual natural interest, which has a great summertime appeal to dwellers of the comparatively monotonous flatlands and of the hot and humid cities. Such advantages, together with its nearness, have caused the region to be developed into what is probably the nation's greatest area of mountain recreation. Thus many lovers of the out-of-doors stay long enough to become acquainted with Longs Peak. Since no one can ride to the summit, and one does not get there by mere hiking but uses hands as aids, it is likely that Longs is the most climbed of any 14,000 foot peak. Because of the ease and safety with which it may be climbed, it offers a wonderful initiation to high-mountain climbing for the ordinary inexperienced person.

While its location has helped to make it famous, that is by no means all. The peak itself has character. It is rugged and severe. It is flanked by distinctive cliffs on all sides instead of by gentle slopes up which roads may be built. Longs Peak dominates. It is a challenge to those with red blood. It is of good repute among skilled climbers. It is never twice alike. The lighting effects, the clouds which hover near it, the storms which play about it, the seasons, and the viewpoints are frequently changing. It is like having a continuous outdoor show for one's amusement, an art gallery for one's appreciation. Whittier truly said,

> *"Touched by a light that hath no name, a glory never sung,*
> *Aloft on sky and mountain wall are God's great pictures hung."*

Longs Peak is higher than Pikes Peak (14,110 ft.) which is only 32nd among Colorado's 54 peaks over 14,000 feet high. Longs Peak itself (14,259 ft.)[1] is 15th among Colorado's host of high mountains which number more than five times as many as the nine contained in the Alps. However, Colorado's highest peak, Mt. Elbert (14,431 ft.), is only 172 feet higher than Longs and has less individuality. All of the other 14,000 foot peaks of the entire Rocky Mountain System are south of Longs Peak in Colorado.

Mt. Whitney (14,495 ft.) in California is the highest peak in the lower forty-eight States of the United States.[2] Like Longs, it has a great precipice on its east face, but it has trails up either side by which one may ride a horse to the very summit. Thirteen other peaks above 14,000 feet are found in California, but no other state has any, except for Mt. Rainier in Washington (14,410 ft.). Compared with Longs, this last is a mile higher above its base. Rainier is more massive, and being in a region of much heavier snowfall, it has 28 glaciers on its flanks. Mt. Rainier thus offers an example of another type of climb on snow and ice with which Longs cannot easily be compared, but neither can such a peak be compared with Longs in regard to rock climbs on walls of granite. Longs Peak is less than half as high as Mt. Everest (29,035 ft.), the highest in the world. Several elevations have changed since the advent of Global Positioning System monitoring; there is now a GPS monitor on the summit of Everest, which records a few millimeters of uplift a year. All elevation figures are given in altitude above sea level.

---

[1] In 2002, the U.S. Geological Survey revised the height of the peak from 14,255 feet to 14,259 feet.
[2] Since Alaska was made a state, Mt. McKinley, 20,320, is now the highest in the 50 states.

Looking toward the Trough
from the Ledges.
Photo by — Lloyd O. Timblin Jr.

The Story of Longs Peak

The story of Longs Peak has many chapters. The longest chapter, if fully told, would be the geologic story. Briefly, Longs was carved out of an older, level-topped mountain, largely by the action of glaciers during the ice age. Working on the four sides, they left four steep faces, separated by four ridges, each of which runs out to a buttressing neighbor peak. Mt. Meeker (13,911), on the southeast ridge, is the highest. Then follow Pagoda (13,491) on the southwest ridge, Storm Peak (13,335) on the northwest ridge, and Mount Lady Washington (13,269) on the northeast ridge. Thus the peak is four-square.

Due to an active glacier and the vertical cleavage of the rocks, Mills Glacier cut the most impressive cirque or chasm on the East Face, leaving a sheer drop of some 1,675 feet and gouging another 600 feet to make a depression for the present Chasm Lake. Such massive solid granite is not volcanic. Neither was it lifted up in a sudden upheaval. The elevation was a slow process through ages of time, and so too has been the carving process, as one can imagine while beholding this impressive sight. "Our mountains are but ruins of former vastly greater mountains," someone has said.

The Indians doubtless had their stories of the peak. They called Longs and Meeker "Nesotaieux" (the Two Guides), for from the south and east the two peaks make a double landmark. The Indians climbed from the south side, or Wild Basin, as related by old Indians who were brought back to the region in 1914 after being away since boyhood. They told of an eagle trap on the top which consisted of a covered pit in which an Indian crouched. Nearby was a stuffed coyote and tallow for bait to attract the eagles, which were seized by the feet and captured for their feathers.

The first white men to see Longs Peak may have been the members of the party of a French trader who reached the base of the mountains on the Platte River July 20, 1799[3]. French traders and trappers were in the region at times thereafter and left their names on some of the streams. Of course, they had a name for the most prominent landmark, for they called Longs and Meeker "Les Deux Oreilles" (the Two Ears).

Major Stephen H. Long's official exploratory expedition is credited with the first written account of viewing Longs Peak on June 30, 1820. They saw it from the plains to the eastward, but continued up the course of the South Platte River and made no close approach. The name Longs Peak appears on maps as early as 1825, but it was not named on the expedition.

In 1864 W. N. Byers and a Mr. Velie made attempts to climb Longs Peak via the Keyhole and via Mt. Meeker, on the summit of which they found the names of five previous climbers. Byers expressed the thought that it would take wings to reach the summit, but four years later he was a member of a party which approached from Grand Lake and finally climbed Longs from the south via the Homestretch as the Indians may have done.

This party was led by Major John W. Powell, one-armed veteran of the Civil War, who the following summer succeeded in making the first boat trip through the Grand Canyon. The group started from Grand Lake. After they had tried the approach over Pagoda and failed, and had established a camp for the night at timberline in Wild Basin, Keplinger, a member of Powell's party, scouted the peak alone. He went through the Notch and made a close approach to the summit, but turned back and did not reach camp until ten o'clock. The next morning the seven reached the top via the Homestretch. The following is taken from Keplinger's account:

> One incident may be mentioned. Major Powell, though one-armed, insisted on doing his stint the same as the rest, even in "packing." At the camp where we left our horses he said, "This is my time to make the bread." I insisted on taking his place, but he would not consent.

[3] *Colorado's Story,* by Dr. Frank C. Spencer, 1930, page 60

I carry with me always the picture of the Major paddling with his one hand in the sticky dough. But he made the biscuits, such as they were. When we put our names in the can, one of these biscuits was put in also, with the statement that this was placed in the can as an everlasting memento to Major Powell's skill in bread making. As we were about to leave the Major thought that was hardly up to the dignity of the occasion, and the biscuit was taken out. We insisted that his real reason was he did not want future generations to know how poor a bread maker so good a mountain climber was. The biscuit was of the kind which when cut with a sharp knife would show a fine-grained, smooth, dark-colored surface. Candor compels me to say that the biscuit would not have been different if he had let me take his place.

As we were about to leave the summit, Major Powell took off his hat and made a little talk. He said, in substance, that we had now accomplished an undertaking in the material or physical field which had hitherto been deemed impossible, but that there were mountains more formidable in other fields of effort which were before us, and he expressed the hope and predicted that what we had that day accomplished was but the augury of yet greater achievements in such other fields.

The first one to feel a continued attachment for Longs Peak was the Rev. Elkanah J. Lamb. In 1871 he climbed the Peak and made the first descent of the East Face (Notch Couloir, Broadway and Lambs Slide) a feat that was repeated only once in the next 50 years (Enos A. Mills in 1903) and by very few others to date. In 1878, Lamb established his home and accommodations for climbers in Tahosa Valley, where Longs Peak Inn now stands. From here he not only guided visitors up Longs Peak at $5 per trip, but rode great distances on horseback to conduct services in various frontier settlements. After seven years his son Carlyle took over the guiding.

Lamb reveled in rugged outdoor living and enjoyed nature in all its moods. As one reads his autobiography and *Miscellaneous Meditations*, one is impressed with the fact that here was a true pioneer who deserves much credit for his early influences.

Enos A. Mills, the famous author and lecturer, purchased the Lamb property in 1902. After it burned in 1906, he rebuilt it in extreme rustic style, using fire-killed timbers of interesting shape and design. Mills made thorough preparations for guiding, including 40 climbs to the top and intensive study of features of interest, before he felt qualified. Then he told of nature along the way so ably and enthusiastically that he came to be known as the father of nature climbing. By his writing and lecturing he did a great deal more to popularize the climb. Furthermore, it was largely through his foresight and efforts that Rocky Mountain National Park itself was established. This resulted in bringing many more visitors to the area and in increasing interest in Longs Peak.

In 1907, Mills, in need of help, selected Shep Husted, W. A. Gray, and Alva Jones as guides. These and many others who followed them carried on Mills' traditions. Shep guided until the middle 30s; he typified everyone's idea of the old-time veteran guide, and conducted famous personages, among them Otis Skinner and Edna Ferber. Husted wrote the following:

Mr. Mills did more to create an interest in mountain climbing than anyone else in the Park. From 1888 to 1906, the years he was guiding, the trips up Longs Peak increased from five or six parties a season to 75 or 80. He created an interest in children climbing the peak and took up a number of small children himself. It is recorded in 1922 that more than a thousand people reached the summit of Longs.

I went to the Inn in 1907 and was with Mr. Mills three summers. He sent me with men to work on the Longs Peak trail when I was not guiding and the trail was practically maintained by Mr. Mills up to the time the national park was created. Mr. Mills made few guiding trips up the peak after 1906, as he was devoting much time to writing. But he trained many peak guides and through his nature talks and his continued development of "nature guiding" on special trips with his guests afield, he aroused in mountain climbers a keener appreciation for the enjoyment of nature.[4]

From 1908 through 1924, Timberline Cabin, initially operated by Enos Mills, served as a stopping point and shelter, or base, for an early start. In late 1926, Boulderfield Shelter Cabin was built by the government, and beginning in 1926, was operated by Robert Collier, Jr., another well-known guide. This gave an opportunity for one to stay over night and become acclimated far up the mountain side for the final climb, which was made in early morning before the frequent mid-day storm. Guides ware also available. By 1936, the stone walls of this building were cracked so badly that it was condemned, and the next year demolished. This was partly due to local melting of persistent ice under the rocks of Boulderfield. The former stable room and rest rooms remained until 1954.

Over 100,000 names have been counted in the summit registers since they were first placed by the Colorado Mountain Club on July 18, 1915. Some test counts indicate that about one-fifth of the climbers were women. As of 1972, 4,064 climbs had been tallied for the East Face. Many more have been made since then, especially since free climbing has become the rule rather than the exception. Most of these climbs have been made since World War II.

Some changes in climbing habits over the years may be noted. In 1915 and 1916 about three-fourths of the climbers went in guided parties and all were by the Keyhole Route. In 1931, at the height of Boulderfield Shelter Cabin days, about one-fourth went with guides and most used the cable route for the ascent. In 1952, guides and their parties accounted for only 11 per cent of the total and over half of the guided trips were by the East Face. There were more moonlight and sunrise parties in the early days, and about 40 percent rode horseback to Boulderfield, whereas about 1 percent do so now. In the first years of definite records, one out of every 220 to 270 who went through the entrances to Rocky Mountain Park climbed to the summit. In 1931, it was one out of every 128. Then the trend started to reverse and in the last few years it was only one out of every 1,000 or so. One may blame this on the increase in automobiles, the discontinuance of Boulderfield Shelter Cabin or anything that one chooses, but it is regrettable that so large a number miss this wonderful experience which many consider as one of the greatest days of their lives.

Over the years there has been a great shift of interest among those guiding and climbing on Longs Peak. Whereas this was once the greatest area of high-mountain, informative nature guiding, the emphasis has now shifted almost entirely to rock climbing in which the peak is again supreme. As Ormes points out, "Longs Peak, and specifically the East Face of the peak, has the nation's greatest concentration of high country rock routes."

The change from mountain appreciation to crevice clinging has not been without some disadvantages. The former had a wider, if more casual, appeal and could not be so directly blamed for various fatalities.

---

[4]Mills, Enos A. *The Rocky Mountain National Park*, pp 59-60. See Bibliography.

Taking a rest on Boulderfield.,

Photo by — *Lloyd O. Timblin Jr.*

Preparation for Climbing

For most, then, the Peak is an object observed from the roads or from a distance. Nevertheless, there is a great deal of interest in what the climb is like and the following pages will attempt to describe it. Those who have no hope of making the actual climb may gain their experience second-hand, while those who expect to climb should be well prepared beforehand.

In addition to reading the suggestions which follow, one should read "Tips and Suggestions," found on page vii of this book. Furthermore, it will be helpful to discuss your climb ahead of time with the ranger on duty at the Ranger Station at the foot of the east trail. The rangers can answer your questions and tell you about snow conditions on the trail at the time.

The most essential preparation is to get in good physical condition. You should not consider Longs Peak until you have made some other high mountain trips. The best way is to start on easy ones and gradually work up to fairly long climbs at high altitudes. Then you will be more sure of yourself and you can really enjoy climbing Longs Peak. Such persons may be contrasted with about one out of ten of those who seriously attempt to reach the summit, but never get there, and an even higher percentage of those who make it, but suffer the discomforts of over-exertion, or mountain sickness, to too great an extent. Conditioning is especially necessary for those who habitually follow the policy, "The Lord is my Shepherd, I shall not walk."

An alternative is to hike part-way, camp overnight, then continue the climb the next morning. There are currently three back country camping locations for this purpose: Goblins' Forest, only a couple of miles up the trail from the ranger station; the Battle Mountain group site, available only to registered groups, and eight campsites at Boulderfield. Back country permits must be obtained (in 2005 they cost $20 per trip for up to seven persons for up to seven nights; see the Rocky Mountain National Park web site, http://www.nps.gov/romo/visit/park/camp/guide.html for current information) from the Backcountry Office near the Park Headquarters. It is good to ask for these sites months in advance, since they are in high demand. The difficulty with this approach is that one hikes more slowly and exerts much more energy carrying a pack, so that a day hike, long as it is, is often a better choice for most people. Overnight campers also tend to ascend the trail later in the day, leaving themselves vulnerable to lightning and high winds on Mills Moraine and at Granite Pass. If you encounter a storm, stay away from ridges and high, exposed areas; descend to forested spots below timberline and wait the storm out, or return to the trail head. The mountain will be there to be climbed another day.

It will be most difficult to make one understand just how hard the trip is, or how easy. You may overestimate or underestimate it, until you have found out by trying. Then it will be hard to tell another, because you are apt to paint it as too hard or too easy depending on how it affected you. The Peak has been climbed by four year olds and by an 85-year-old. It was climbed by Mrs. E. J. Lamb when she was 70. It has been climbed by a paraplegic and by two blind women. At age 63, H. L. Higby, guide, climbed on foot all of the way from Hewes-Kirkwood on three successive days and got all members of his parties to the top.

Only a few have ever been seriously injured by a fall or a slip on the regular routes during the summer climbing season. However, one's hands will be needed and probably knees for steep pitches. Some will consider themselves uncomfortably close to the edge of great drops, but they will get along all right like thousands of others. The illustrations show, of course, the most spectacular and difficult places. One does not need to hang over great drops with only scanty hand and foot holds, nor does one even need to look over an edge. Some have partly spoiled their trip by being overly concerned beforehand, and then they have found out that the bad places are not nearly so bad as imagined. It is perfectly all right to trim your toenails the night before. You won't have to hang on that tight.

More frequent difficulties are found in adjusting to the altitude or summoning sufficient endurance to make the climb and return home, a long way back when one is exhausted. Taking your own experience into account, you must make up your own mind about climbing. If a physically handicapped person and an 85-year-old can do it and walk all of the way, you should at least be able to do it with the help of a horse, that is, if you have not let your body age far beyond your years. The Peak is not that hard; the difficulty lies in the poor physical condition of many who attempt it. It is a great experience and you may be sorry that you missed it. It will be worth the effort and the day will be well spent, even if you turn back before reaching the top. You should be willing to turn back rather than delay the rest of the party.

There are two regular routes to the end of the horse trail on Boulderfield, and one route from Boulderfield to the summit by which one climbs over the rocks on foot, without benefit of constructed trail.

One of the horse trails starts north of the peak at the Glacier Gorge Parking Area on the Bear Lake Road about a mile below Bear Lake. It follows the Loch Vale Trail for a mile or more and then branches to the left. It climbs through miles of forest land burnt over by the great fire of 1900, and emerges above timberline on the slopes of Battle Mountain. Following these slopes, it joins the other trail at Granite Pass, after which the route for the two trails is the same for the remaining mile and a half to the end of the constructed trail on Boulderfield. This north trail starts at an elevation of about 9,200 feet and its length to Boulderfield is 8.9 miles. It is much less popular, longer, and has less variety and interest along the way.

The other trail starts east of the Peak at the Longs Peak Ranger Station at an elevation of 9,530 feet and is 5.9 miles to the center of Boulderfield. *See the maps page 23 and on back cover.*

In addition to deciding which trail is more convenient to take, you should decide whether or not to ride horses and if you should take a guide. Horses can be taken (contact Sombrero Ranch's Allenspark Stables, 303-747-2551; they charge approximately $150 per horse for a ride to Boulderfield, climb to the top, then a ride back down; they leave the trail head with a wrangler at 3 a.m. by pre-arrangement), and can save your energy so that you may enjoy the final climb to a greater extent, and also make the long trip home more easily. Furthermore, they will allow you to see much more as you ride, for you do not need to watch your feet and the trail so closely. Since the trail is all up or down hill, the usual pace is a walk, which is not nearly so liable to make a novice stiff and sore. If a good equestrian takes the lead, the other horses will usually follow without any difficulty unless they find that their riders will let them loaf or eat along the way. If so, a contest will ensue to see who is boss. It is best to make them keep up from the start and not let them get any ideas.

At Boulderfield, the horses should be tied with the halter ropes provided, their bridles should be removed and hung over the saddle horn, and their cinches should be loosened. Before mounting for the return, you must be sure that the cinches are re-tightened, and that the animal doesn't have a chance to take off down the trail before the bridle is on. From this it will be seen that if you takes horses, a wrangler or a guide will be helpful to have along.

A guide to the top is of value for added safety, for knowing the best climbing pace, for saving time in many ways, for peace of mind, and for information which can be imparted along the way. Parties without guides often go too fast at the start and several members play out before they get to the top, or else the party may enjoy the day and their rests too much and find themselves returning after dark The guide is in charge of the party and should be obeyed. The guide should set the pace and that means no one should get ahead unless invited to do so. Neither should anyone drop out of the party until consulting the guide and getting instructions as to what to do. The above remarks apply concerning the leader of any party, whether a professional guide or a friend with more experience who has been up before. The National Park Service issues permits to qualified guides and will supply up-to-date information concerning them and their rates.

The trip to Chasm Lake is in itself a wonderful experience and enough of an outing for many. There, the rock-bound setting makes one feel in a world apart and provides some feeling of the austere nature and greatness of Longs Peak. Although one cannot ride all of the way to Chasm Lake, it can be combined as a side trip with a horseback ride ending at Boulderfield.

Rangers at the Longs Peak Ranger Station or the Backcountry Office near Park Headquarters can tell you the nearest places where saddle horses can be rented. A wrangler guide, as distinguished from a climbing guide, will accompany horseback parties. They are not permitted to go beyond Chasm Lake Junction or Boulderfield.

Arrangements for guides and horses should be made in advance and should include an understanding of what is to be done in case of unfavorable weather before the starting time. Mountain weather is changeable and hard to predict, and especially when reservations and several people are involved, it is generally best to make a start as planned and see what develops. A gloomy morning may be the prelude to a wonderful day above the clouds. John Kiernan said, "Bad weather always looks much worse through a window." However, those who are climbing independently or are planning a difficult route would be wise to wait for a better day.

About ninety-nine per cent of climbers make the entire trip on foot either for economy or by preference. A good hiker can make better time than the average horseback party. Furthermore, it is easier to stop for pictures or to converse along the way. A guide is not needed by persons with some mountain experience if this book serves a purpose for which it is intended, or especially if one goes with someone who has been up before. It is quite likely that from the middle of July until Labor Day there will be other climbing parties within sight in case one needs assistance. Furthermore, special rangers are assigned to look after Longs Peak and its climbers.

Starting time is another important factor to be planned ahead. Although the trip may be made in eight or ten hours, the average time is probably nearly 11 hours. Harold Dunning reports being out over 18 hours with one party and Cliff Higby reports that it took him and his father (both guides) 24 hours to get one man to the top and back. One should also consider the summer weather, which is frequently clear in the morning but develops a thunderstorm by mid-afternoon. It is thus to one's advantage to reach the summit before a storm develops. Not only will you be more comfortable and have a better view, but the danger from lightning is lessened. Taking these things into account, one can see the advisability of an early start and should leave the trail head by 3 a.m., if at all possible. Believe it or not, as of this writing, parking can be a problem even this early. And sudden changes in weather on the peak cannot be underestimated. Leave early (Daylight Saving Time used throughout).

One's equipment should include comfortable, stout shoes with low heels. Much of the difficulty which some people have in crossing the uneven rocks of Boulderfield is due to improper footwear. One should obtain shoes that are large enough for two pairs of socks and so that the foot can accommodate itself to different slanting positions upon the rocks. Shoes or boots with rubber lug soles are best for nearly all climbing conditions. Leather soles are dangerously slippery.

Additional equipment should include a jacket or raincoat which will shed water, gloves for wet, cold rocks when it storms, a hat for protection from hail and rain, for shading the eyes, and for protecting the face from the fiercely burning rays of the sun, dark glasses, and warm enough clothes for a cold wind or storm. However, you should not over-burden yourself with clothes. Saddle slickers are furnished with horses, but they are too cumbersome to carry beyond Boulderfield, and too long for climbing over the rocks in safety. No matter what one takes, the day may bring cold moments when you wish you had more, and yet most of the day you may be warm and wish you had less to carry. You should usually climb in no more than one shirt and avoid perspiration which may chill you in the cold wind at the summit after you have ceased to exert yourself.

Some member of the party should carry a first aid kit and flashlight. A sunburn preparation on the face, and perhaps the hands, before one starts will be of more aid than after one gets back. Someone has written,

> *The girl who incandescent glows*
> *Where sun and rain have kissed her,*
> *Is less alluring to her beaux*
> *When she begins to blister.*

You should get up in time to eat breakfast leisurely. If you drive to the foot of the trail, or if you ride horseback, you will have time for breakfast to be quite well digested before high altitude and exertion stop the process. However, if you are to start hiking right after eating, it is better to eat a light breakfast. Even though you may feel quite empty on the upward trail, it is better to save the lunch until the summit is reached. Your body will have enough to do to get there without having to digest food along the way. Hard sugar candy which needs no digestion may be carried for quick energy and eaten en route. Trail mix or other light snacks will help too.

A sack lunch should be taken, but its contents may vary a great deal because of individual preferences. Until you have found that you can eat well on a hard climb, it is better to take a light lunch. There is no water on top and something in liquid form or juicy fruit may be enjoyed. At the edge of Boulderfield, one may find small streams from sources to the left but they are not suitable for drinking unless brought to boiling or filtered. There are now lightweight, portable filters on the market which filter out Giardia lamblia, a parasite found in Park water which can produce painful if not fatal symptoms. On day hikes, hikers should carry adequate clean water with them. Camping overnight at Boulderfield usually means you will have to boil or filter water from the streams flowing through the boulders to have enough. When climbing, be careful not to drink too much water at any one time; pace yourself, so you do not get dehydrated or drink more than you need.

One should not attempt the climb alone and it is well to avoid large parties. The party should be kept together, or else definitely split with an understanding about what each group intends to do. Until such an agreement is reached, it is the responsibility of the faster members of the party to hold themselves back to the pace of the slower members. They should not allow themselves to get ahead and then have to wait. It is imperative that no slow member be left behind and alone on the return trip.

The Trail to Boulderfield

Now we are ready to start. We shall meet early at the Longs Peak parking area and get acquainted. Reference may be made to the map and the illustrations as we climb along. This armchair trip is guaranteed not to make muscles sore, nor blister a nose, and it is hoped that it will make it easy for many to enjoy the trip whether or not they can actually climb.

At the foot of the trail there is a register box where we are asked to leave our names, the time, our route and destination. This information is of aid to the Longs Peak Ranger in case of real or supposed emergency. We should not fail to "sign out" on the register and write down the time of day as we return.

About two and a half miles up the trail we emerge from the thick forest into an area burned by a forest fire in 1900. If the day is clear, dark glasses should be donned, for the air is thin and the sun's rays are brilliant without the shade of the trees to break their glare. Timberline conditions are now in evidence, for the slope ahead was so wind-swept, even before the fire, that the trees were unable to grow straight. The grotesque skeletons still stand, twisted and gnarled, weird ghosts of the former "struggling" forest. Of particular interest are the two erect, but short, banner trees close to the left of the trail. The strong, prevailing westerly winds have permitted only the branches on the eastward, lee side, to grow. Look between them as you pass by to get the full effect.

From this windswept hill, we get our first good view of the plains beyond the foothills. The town of Longmont (pop. 76,098 in 2002) may be discerned as a dark patch to the right of Twin Sisters Mountain. Also visible by reflected morning light are several lakes or reservoirs.

Some distance beyond the next switchback, the trail passes through a sheltered hollow a bit deeper than one's height, A glance at the crest of this hollow shows dwarfed aspen trees and sub-alpine fir with blunt needles. A study of other nearby shrubs and shrubby growths reveals limber pine with needles in bunches of five, Engelmann spruce with single, stiff, sharp needles, alpine birch with round bright shiny leaves, an alpine willow with longer pale green leaves, and stubby cinquefoil with small leaves subdivided into five leaflets. Elsewhere dwarf juniper might be seen. These are the trees and shrubs which one is likely to find at timberline on Longs Peak. Watch and listen here too for the white-crowned sparrow who says, "I'm GLAD you-came-to-see-me."

Just beyond this little hollow, the wind has swept the ground quite barren of trees and shrubs except for one prostrate limber pine to the left, which has been able to start in the shelter of a small boulder. This tree is perhaps 12 feet long but only 18 inches high and has been wind-trimmed like a hedge and conforms to the shape of the rock. It shows how constant is the direction of the strong winds. It is like a grave with its headstone. How would you like to lie in such a grave with the wind for a constant caretaker, and continually whispering about far off places or loudly informing you of the weather?

A short distance beyond, a trail turns to the right and crosses Alpine Brook toward the site of the former Timberline Cabin and then turns westward toward Jim's Grove. We shall take the left branch, following the regular trail up Mills Moraine and get the wonderful views of the East Face and the great chasm in the morning light as we move toward them.

As we approach the moraine we may spot several additional examples of trees trimmed to fit the rocks which shelter them. At the crest of the moraine, we look down its steeper slope beyond, which was in contact with the ancient glacier. A thousand feet below, the rather broad valley floor drained by Roaring Fork is a jumble of huge boulders left in irregular heaps by the retreating glacier. Across the gorge may be seen, but less distinctly, the other lateral moraine left on the opposite flank of the glacier. These moraines are the ridges of ground-up rocks and boulders, which were carved from the mountainside and carried and pushed aside to their present position by a huge mass of glacial ice which filled, and slowly moved along the valley.

Look ahead at the chasm carved from the flanks of Longs Peak and Mt. Meeker. There was the catchment basin where wind piled the snow in the shelter of the Peaks. There it settled, packed to ice, and moved downward, tearing away rocks and grinding them as it did so. There it left the great chasm or cirque as it diminished. Do not fail sometime to take the left-hand trail at the fork ahead and visit Chasm Lake. The foot trail stops at the site of the former Chasm Lake Shelter Cabin, 200 or 300 feet below the lake (on March 23, 2003, an avalanche destroyed the Cabin; it was rebuilt later in 2003). One then climbs on foot, following a break in the rocks leading upward behind the cabin. It is doubtful if any lake rests in a more awe-inspiring setting (*photo page 47*). Chasm Lake cannot be seen from the trail, but one can see Peacock Pool from near the trail fork, and above the lake is Columbine Falls. We should be on Mills Moraine by five or six o'clock.

Boulderfield approach to the Keyhole.

Photo by — Lloyd O. Timblin Jr.

Alpine Life

Continuing to the right of the Longs Peak Trail, we soon come to a greener swale along the side of Mount Lady Washington where rivulets of water trickle across the trail. Watch here and the rest of the way to Boulderfield for the Ptarmigan, a small grouse-like bird colored and mottled so nearly like the granite boulders strewn about, that it is likely to just sit and let you go by unseeing. In winter they are white and protectively colored against the snow. Watch also from here on for the Pipit or Wagtail, a small buff-colored bird which shows light outer tail feathers when it flies. Possibly here, but more likely farther on, will be found the Rosy Finch, a brownish sturdy little bird with dark rose showing on the shoulders and rump.

These birds, and the plants among the rocks, are arctic-alpine. That is, they live on the mountain tops above timberline (alpine) and also in identical or similar forms in the arctic regions beyond timberline to the northward, where the climatic conditions are similar in regard to severity. Carl Sharsmith aptly expressed the thought that our mountain tops are climatic islands of arctic life and conditions. You have traveled the equivalent of a long way north since you had your breakfast.

Here too we should begin to watch for the Cony and the Yellow-bellied Marmot. The Cony, or Pika, is like a six-inch rabbit but with round ears and no tail. It is likely to be seen scampering among the rocks, or more likely to be noticed sitting on a rock, while its metallic warning squeak is heard. In late season, one may be seen carrying a mouthful of green foliage to cure and place in his hay pile for winter use. The Marmot, or mountain form of Ground Hog, may attract our attention by its sharp, loud warning whistle. It is grizzled brown, larger than a cat, and has a bushy tail and an awkward gait. It may be seen even on the very top of Longs Peak

Tiny, brilliant alpine flowers may cover the ground between the boulders, but they are too numerous to discuss here. Many of them grow in low mats such as the Alpine Pink, colored true to its name, the blue Alpine Phlox, and the white Sandwort, all with numerous tiny blossoms. A yellow, five-petaled flower, the Alpine Avens, grows in larger clumps and on stems which may be six inches tall. So also does the Alpine Sunflower, a blossom of which may be three inches across and that far above the ground. The flowers that one sees will depend upon the time of season, for their blooming period is short. The alpine flowers are best about the second week in July and are quite gone on the drier slopes by the third week in August.

The trail crosses the north ridge of Mount Lady Washington next to Battle Mountain at Granite Pass. Here it is joined by the trail from the Bear Lake side and here we get our next great change of view, for now we see the eastern slopes of the Front or Rampart Range and of the Mummy Range. Bearing to the left, we ascend the slope toward Longs Peak. After a few zigzags, we are able to see the North Face of Longs Peak across the comparatively level upland basin called Boulderfield. Countless boulders of all sizes are strewn about. We should aim to be here by six or seven a.m.

Boulderfield

The trail winds among the boulders to the very center of the area and stops at a hitching rack for ten or twelve horses. Nearby was a telephone and a sealed chest of equipment for emergency use only. This was the site of the former Boulderfield Shelter Cabin, rest rooms and stable, now crumbled by the elements. To the left, or eastward, the rocky

Colliers Hotel and Stables, Boulderfield.
Photo courtesy — Helen Hannen Donahue

surface of Boulderfield turns upward to the summit of Mount Lady Washington. We have come around this mountain and are now behind it as compared with our starting point. To the right or westward is Storm Peak. Just to the left of the low place between Storm Peak and Longs Peak, a huge rock overhanging from the left forms the Keyhole. Ahead lies the summit of Longs Peak a mile away. At times one may see a climber on top silhouetted against the sky. To the left of the summit is the top of the East Face, as smooth and as perpendicular as if a great knife had sliced away a section. There, at the point where the view of the East Face is cut off by the ridge which connects with Mount Lady Washington, is Chasm View.

Climbers before July, 1973, had their choice of two routes. The North Face offered the more direct way by what was called the Cable Route. The most usual climb was to go up this way and down via the Keyhole. This route offered a "round trip" via the North Face and the summit. The Wilderness Preservation Act of 1964 mandated the removal of all man-made contrivances other than those designated "historical," so the cables had to go. A danger of the North Face consists in the ice and snow which may cover a part of the way in early or late season. Even without this hazard, now that the cables are gone and only a few bolts remain, the North Face is a technical climb, and should be attempted only by trained, experienced climbers with appropriate equipment. **DO NOT ATTEMPT THIS ROUTE UNLESS YOU ARE SO QUALIFIED; TECHNICAL CLIMBING CAN BE FATAL.**

A very serious injury from a slip and fall occurred on a North Face snow bank. The following quotation from the *Estes Park Trail* of July 25, 1947, tells the story:

> A distance of three feet in either direction would have meant a fall of 1,000 feet and certain death for Donald Davidson of Staten Island, New York, last Monday morning, when, with Mrs. Davidson, he was climbing the North Face of Longs Peak.
>
> The two, both inexperienced mountain climbers, according to Park service officials, were near the second cable when Davidson lost his hold and slid over a snow bank. Just at the edge of a precipice, with a drop of 1,000 feet below, Davidson hit a rock, the only one in the area.
>
> He suffered a broken shoulder and was in so much pain he was unable to make the trip down the Peak unaided. Mrs. Davidson went for help . . .
>
> Five rangers, led by Acting Chief Ranger Ernest Field, left immediately for the scene of the accident.
>
> Upon reaching the injured man, it was found necessary to carry him on a stretcher to the Boulderfield, where he was placed on a horse for the remainder of the trip to the Longs Peak ranger station, and finally brought to the Estes Park hospital for treatment, about 8 p.m. Monday evening.

The present route proceeds through the Keyhole; the route turns to the left where we cannot see it on the west side of the Peak and traverses the Ledges or Shelf where one climbs up for a time, and then has to descend and lose altitude, the bane of all mountain climbers. The way ascends again in the long Trough, turns the corner to the south side of the Peak, goes along the Narrows, and finally up the Home Stretch to the top. This route is perhaps a half mile longer in distance and an hour longer in climbing time than the more direct way up the North Face. It gives one more variety of viewpoints and is now the only recommended route for non-technical climbers to use.

We start on slowly, especially if we have ridden horses, for in that case we are less adjusted to the high altitude. The way is now more difficult for there is no trail. We simply pick our own route as we go, over boulders and around them. We are unaccustomed to such walking and we are likely to hold ourselves too tense as we try to balance ourselves on the irregular surfaces or edges of the boulders. We should therefore give our attention to relaxing and holding ourselves down to a leisurely pace or we shall soon be breathless. Long and high steps should be avoided for they take more energy and make it more difficult to keep your balance. Just relax and mosey along like a Sunday afternoon stroll. We'll save time and energy in the long run, for we shall not wear ourselves out so fast, nor need to rest so much. Rests should be for short pauses only, preferably without sitting down, and without cooling the body.

You can relax a bit after each step. It is a mountain-climbing trick that you will not master for several climbs, but it will give you all of the rest that you need as you go along. It is comparable to one's heart, which rests a sizeable fraction of the time, but instead of stopping for a few hours to rest, it rests a bit after each beat and so may keep working steadily day and night for a century. Step and relax, step and relax, on we go.

Since we are not all experts, we shall pause now and then, keeping the party together. "Steady wins the race. See how far we have come? Well, let's have another spasm." And so on runs the guide's patter.

The Rocks of the Peak

At the next pause, the guide may start with, "There are two kinds of rocks here: granites and schists. The schists are the darker colored, banded rocks. When the bands are close together as in these, they may be called schists, but if they are more coarsely banded, they may be called gneiss (pronounced just like "nice"). Schist and gneiss. One is schist as gneiss as the other!"

The group moves on as the guide continues. "This schist is metamorphic rock. It is made over; it was deep within the surface of the earth and great heat and pressure was applied to make it tend to run together or re-melt. In still earlier times it may have been old sediments or old volcanic rock. Take a good look. You may never have seen any rocks that were older.

"The schist was here before the granite. That reddish piece there is granite. See, it is granular. It is made up mostly of crystals of quartz and feldspar. The granite came in here as a molten mass in pre-Cambrian time and cooled deep beneath the surface. This is known because of the size of the crystals. It takes a long time for the molecules to arrange themselves in such crystals. In general, the slower the cooling, the larger the crystals. This granite is porphyritic, which means that some of the crystals are distinctly larger

Banded schist.

Photo by — Lloyd O. Timblin Jr.

than the ground mass. In this case, there are well-formed feldspar crystals which show Carlsbad twinning as longitudinal divisions on the broken surfaces.

"See those great streaks of dark schist in the wall there ahead of us? See that area where the granite welled in and took over? See there where it pushed in between layers of schist? When that was done, it took great pressure because it was under layers of rock at considerable depth. Since then, this whole region has been lifted, not in any great upheaval, but in a long slow process, perhaps with many slips and earthquakes. As it was being raised, weather and erosion were constantly at work upon it. They have removed the top layers, carved out the mountains, and exposed the old core which we now see. It has taken about 60 million years to make these mountains. If they had raised steadily, that would take less then one inch per century to raise them more than twice as high as they now stand. Old levels were formed when the uplifting processes rested a few million years, and then the glaciers took over the last bit sculpturing contract. It is a long story and might be made much longer, but meanwhile we have gone a long way up this mountain."

After answering a few questions, the guide starts in all over. "There are two kinds of rocks around here — big ones and little ones. 'Nuf said."

Perhaps some climber makes a wisecrack like "I sure feel sheepish climbing over these rocks — mountain sheepish."

At Chasm View

The Cable Route involved hiking over the boulders to the extreme left, toward the saddle between Mt. Lady Washington and the North Face. You may still do this to get to Chasm View, a spot from which you may see a spectacular sight: the great sheer granite East Face and the chasm below (*photo page 27*). This will add considerable time and energy to your climb, so you must judge accordingly whether you can spare the exertion. Most will want to go over the boulders directly to the Keyhole, the prominent notch just to the left of the saddle connecting Longs Peak and Storm Peak, the mountain which looks like Mt. Lady Washington's twin across Boulderfield on the west side.

If you decide to make the effort, you can climb along a few ledges and look over the edge at Chasm View. You not only look over, but up as well at the great wall rising above. You are somewhat nearer the top than the bottom of this great precipice. Below is Broadway, a ledge which extends across the cliff. It is used in climbing the East Face.

At the foot of the declivity lies a body of snow and ice, hardly a glacier, yet often called Mills Glacier. Far below and to the left is Chasm Lake, a deep, dark pool some thousand feet across. Between the ice and the lake is a quarter mile of broken rock, partly the work of the glacier, and partly the talus slope of debris tumbled down as a result of the attacks of weather upon the mighty cliff. Chasm Lake was gouged out by the glacier and is in no way a crater lake as once thought.

There is a convenient rock, like a wall, over which you may have leaned as you looked straight down. Then as you start along the edge toward the north face, you notice that a crack has opened, down which you can look and see green growth some 500 feet below. This reveals that the edge is overhanging and being loosened from the main cliff. Play safe and stay away from the edge, especially with large parties. Tom Hornbein, who has climbed directly underneath Chasm View, reports that there is a large adjacent block just to the left or east which appears particularly unsafe and should be avoided. Light may be seen through the fissure between it and the main body of rock. Don't be the fool that rushes out where climbers fear to tread.

If you have gone to Chasm View, you must now proceed across the boulders to the Keyhole. While you are proceeding to the Keyhole, let your eye follow the ridge to the left, or east, to another notch, the False Keyhole. This smaller notch has been the downfall of some climbers returning from the summit, who mistake it for the true Keyhole and get lured out onto its dangerous ledges. Mark this shape and location for future reference on your return trip from the summit, when you will be watching for it on the other side of the ridge. Avoid this pitfall on the return, and watch for the Park Service sign that points along the Ledges to the true Keyhole.

At the Keyhole is a point of decision. The group is far enough along so that the leader should have been able to size up the individual members of the party. The leader should also take into account the time of day, the weather and the snow and ice conditions ahead. A decision should be made whether or not all of the party can make the climb without undue discomfort or delay. If you leave the Keyhole after 8 a.m., it is late, unless the day is still fair.

Having reached a conclusion, the leader may give some words of advice and explanation. Pointing to the route ahead and indicating its nature, well chosen words can discourage or encourage certain members of the party. Now would be the time to turn back if anyone feels discouraged. By doing so they will not inconvenience the party nor delay it. They can rest awhile and then make their way back to Boulderfield below, even alone. However, if they go on, the leader must either "drag" them on to the top, or may want to have someone accompany them back at least to the Keyhole, for no one who becomes nervous or physically miserable should return alone.

If the guide believes that some persons should turn back, he or she may then let them proceed with the clear understanding that it is against recommendations, or may compel them to return. However, the times when compulsion is resorted to should be rare. The first death on the Peak resulted when a woman insisted on going on against the better judgment of her guide. The writer once asked Shep Husted how he handled such cases and Shep replied about as follows: "Oh, I just talk them out of it. I ask them how they are feeling and suggest that they look a little white around the gills. I ask them what they had for breakfast, and shake my head, and after a time, they at least imagine that they are sick and drop out."

When someone does turn back, it is necessary to have a clear understanding of just what he or she will do. Since such persons may slow the party on the return, and since their wait is liable to be long and cold, it is better for them to work their way back in a leisurely manner. It is important on the return to be sure that they are ahead, so they must be cautioned to stay on the main trail. In addition, they may leave word or a signal at certain key points to show that they have passed by. The round building with the conical roof just at the Keyhole is the Agnes Vaille Memorial Shelter (see later description of the Agnes Vaille tragedy, p. 40). Because of

The Keyhole.

Photo by — Lloyd O. Timblin Jr.

the Wilderness Preservation Act, in order to render the Shelter nothing more than an historical landmark, the door has been removed. Nevertheless, the building may still provide a welcome place to rest.

At the Keyhole, it is not unusual to encounter ferocious winds, sometimes in excess of 50 to 60 miles an hour. Some climbers may be put off by these winds, and decide not to venture farther. Use your own judgment; remember, though, that the wind is always worst at the Keyhole, and that beyond, on the Ledges, it will not be as bad.

The view of Glacier Gorge from the Keyhole is splendid, and is well worth the hike, even if you do not venture on to the summit. There is a detailed description of this in the section on the view from the summit. The many lakes and mountains across the gorge and the view north to the Trail Ridge Road area on a clear day is breathtaking.

From the Keyhole, turn down and left to the Ledges. There are red and yellow blazes painted on the rocks marking the way. Look carefully for these, and stay on the marked routes as closely as possible. For a time, there was a plan to let these blazes wear off the rocks to eliminate yet another sign of human presence. The National Park Service Solicitation Office has determined that the blazes must stay, since the public expects them; this is an important decision, since in a few steps you can easily get off the established route and end up at a dead-end or worse. FOLLOW THE MARKED ROUTE!

The Ledges *(see photo page 2)* travel across the West Face of Longs to a couloir called the Trough. On a typical day during the summer climbing season, the Trough will be full of climbers. The Trough is somewhat similar to Boulderfield in that it is full of small rocks and boulders, and requires some actual hand-over-hand climbing in places. The loose rock can present a real hazard to climbers below.

Not only should you refrain from the adolescent stunt of starting rocks in order to see them bound down the slope, but you should be sure that your feet or hands do not start loose rocks unintentionally. Just ahead it is steep enough that if a rock starts, it could gain momentum as it bounds downward. It in turn may start others. If rocks come down from above, and you cannot get under an overhang for protection, then you must watch them continuously and dodge as best you can. By climbing conveniently close behind one another, each person can usually stop a rock which may be started by the climber just ahead before it gains momentum.This will greatly lessen the danger when the party is large. Fortunately much "gardening" (loose rock removal) has already been done, so do not let fear spoil your fun. Mountain climbing is like life. If you worry about all of the hazards ahead, you ruin it. Just take it a step at a time.

Mountain Sickness

And "Oh boy," that mountain sickness! It usually starts with a headache which proceeds into dizziness and nausea, and may result in losing whatever is in your stomach. It is like sea sickness, except that instead of feeding the fishes, one can only nourish the scenery. It is caused by insufficient oxygen in the body, which in turn is caused by the rare air of high altitude, together with the body's demands for extra oxygen due to exertion. We never have enough oxygen or blood for all of our organs to be active at once. In climbing at high altitudes our muscles demand so much oxygen that the head and stomach, for example, have little left. You may feel light-headed, and may empty your stomach. The body of a person who gets mountain sickness is simply not able to adjust itself to the demands put upon it either due to lack of adaptability, or simply to poor physical condition. When you live long enough in high altitude to acclimate yourself, your blood develops more red corpuscles. Though each corpuscle must carry less oxygen at high altitudes, the greater number makes up for the deficiency.

When you are on the mountain top, it is too late to do much but suffer the discomforts. Rest helps, but afterwards the air is just as rare as it was before. To climb down takes more exertion, but it has to be done, in varying degrees of misery by the suffering patients, and with much patience by the other members of the group. Some recover quite well when they get below what for them is their critical altitude. Others may have a headache until after they have fallen asleep that night.

Mountain sickness has its many humorous angles. Someone said that he was feeling rather low to be so high. Someone else said, "Well, if there is anything in a person, mountain climbing will sure bring it out." One may be said to join the Daniel Boone Club; that is, he goes out and shoots his lunch. There are three states: first, a person is afraid that he is going to die; second, he gets so that he doesn't care if he does; and finally, he is afraid that he is not going to die.

"What should I do," asked the solicitous wife, "if John gets mountain sickness?"

"Don't worry. He'll do it," was the answer.

The story is told that when one fellow was in the process of losing his lunch, he was asked, "What's the matter? Is your stomach weak?"

The unfortunate fellow took another verifying look over the edge and reported,

"Nope, I guess I'm throwing it about as far as anyone ever did."

The best course of action for mountain sickness on a mountain top are a slow pace with rests, and administration of aromatic spirits of ammonia ("Acrobatic spirits of come-on-ya"). A few drops in part of a cup of water may be taken internally, or, lacking convenient water, you may wet your tongue with it, smell the bottle or an inhalant capsule, or rub the liquid on your upper lip for convenient and continued smelling. Sometimes you may help a natural process by lying over a rock and tickling the back of your throat. Perhaps most important of all is to refrain from eating. Let the guide have your lunch. He or she may enjoy it. On feeling a headache, some are prone to take aspirin. It is this guide's experience that it only aggravates the case. Let it alone. Practice consciously taking two or three deep breaths for each step. This may help more than anything.

Dr. Henry Buchtel, M.D., an experienced Colorado climber and leader says, "The use of alcohol at any time during the trip cannot be too strongly condemned; its use means only trouble for the entire party."

In regard to climbing mountains, folks may be divided into four classes: those who do not even try; those who try, but do not get to the top; those who get to the top, but cannot eat their lunch; and those who get to the top and also enjoy their lunch.

On to the Summit

At the top of the Trough you reach the legendary Narrows (*photo page 38*). With its narrow trail and sheer drops, this stretch can be frightening for the faint-hearted. For those afraid of heights, not looking down and concentrating on the trail ahead helps, as does the presence of calmer and steadier companions. It is encouraging to note that the part of the Narrows nearest the Trough is the narrowest place, so once you are beyond that, the trail widens and is not so unsettling. Horseplay, or making light of this spot, is unwise; you should concentrate on the trail ahead and on keeping your balance. Just in case you are tempted to take all this too lightly, nature has placed an ominous looking large black boulder, aptly called "The Hearse," at the foot of the canyon.

Top of the Trough.

Photo by — Lloyd O. Timblin Jr.

At the end of the Narrows is the final ascent, a feature called the Home Stretch. These cracked, slanting slabs of granite are more formidable on the descent. One will usually want to ascend on all fours, and descend, as William Allen White put it, "on all fives." If there are other climbers on the Home Stretch when you arrive, as there invariably are, you will note that generally one route is taken on the ascent, while another is used for the descent. Follow the crowd. Soon you will be filled with a sense of satisfaction and accomplishment, as you stand on the summit of one of the Rockies' highest peaks!

Storms and Clouds

The time spent on top can literally be an hour of heaven when the day is mild and clear, or it can be a few moments of fog, storm, and chattering teeth. It may even be a time of danger on rare occasions when lightning is striking. At such times it is best to gauge your time with the approaching storm and remain on the lee side of the Peak until the storm has abated, or else carefully hurry down ahead of it. Usually the storms come from the west, which make the western rim and ridges most hazardous. Fortunately the trails do not follow ridges to any great extent. Thunderstorms are likely to occur on the way home, so be wary around the edge of Boulderfield, near Granite Pass, and on Mills Moraine. If you should find yourself in the neighborhood of lightning strikes, you should get into the closest depression and lie down. Do not stay on a horse. Neither may it be safe to lead it. Tether the horse as best you can, perhaps by laying a large rock on the end of the reins. Then withdraw, always down hill, and wait, and hope your horse does too.

Occasionally one encounters the phenomenon of discharging static electricity. The Peak acts as a point of discharge for the surface of the earth and electricity flows into the air upon the approach of a thunderstorm. The discharge may make one's hair stand up, or it may be strong enough to cause a crackling or buzzing sound especially from metal objects, but also about one's head or an upraised finger. Although it may be followed by a storm, it is often of short duration and in itself is harmless. The experience, however, is memorable and incites great interest. Rev. Lamb wrote of "reveling in the luxury of an electric bath at the expense of nature." Nevertheless, it is a warning of a dangerous situation. Lie down on the side of the summit, or of a projection, which is away from the direction from which the storm is approaching, or start hiking down.

The usual storms bring only fleeting discomforts that would soon be forgotten except that one likes to tell about them. To have weathered a storm is an added attraction of the climb. You should really be disappointed if you do not encounter a summer snow storm, for most of the precipitation at that altitude is snow or snow pellets. The experience makes you more closely in tune with the elements and more appreciative of the sheltered existence in which you usually live. Perhaps during a storm the group will enjoy singing the refrain, "You freeze a jolly good fellow." Or perhaps they will appreciate having the Biblical expression paraphrased, "Many are cold, but few are frozen."

Views and Doings On Top

Looking West over Glacier Gorge to McHenrys Peak.

Photo by — Lloyd O. Timblin Jr.

Heavenly days on the top are those when the sun is shining and one can see for miles and miles: to Pikes Peak 103 miles south in a straight line, to Mt. Evans, the Arapahoes, Fair Glacier, Grays and Torreys Peaks, Mt. Massive, Mt. of the Holy Cross, the Gore Range, Middle Park, the Flattops away over west, the Park Range, the Never Summer Mountains, the Medicine Bow Range into Wyoming, to mention the more notable or prominent features; in addition, there are numerous closer summits, valleys, gorges, and lakes. On a clear day, the level horizon of the Great Plains may show clearly, with closer dark patches visible for Denver, Longmont, Loveland, Fort Collins and Greeley. At night you can see the lights of these cities, smaller towns, and numerous car headlights.

The distance to the horizon is about 120 miles. This is figured according to the formula which takes into account the earth's curvature: distance seen in miles equals the square root of the three halves of the difference in altitude. This latter figure is somewhat less than 10,000 feet. The total distance seen reaches about two-thirds of the way to Kansas. It is possible to see into Nebraska and easy to see into Wyoming, but one may see only a bit more than halfway into Utah and less than halfway into New Mexico. The complete circle of visible land seen from the top of Longs is somewhat larger than the state of Ohio. If Longs Peak were placed near Columbus, Ohio, one could see into all of the neighboring states and Lake Erie. Placed at Philadelphia, one could see from Connecticut to Washington, D.C., if the air were ever clear enough in that region.

Seeing the distant view from the top is only one of the enjoyable things to do. You should not fail to peer down at Chasm Lake from the northeast edge of the summit. You may go to the western edge of the four-acre, flat, but rocky, top of the Peak, and look down on Glacier Gorge. However, if pressed for time, you will get the same view as you descend the Trough.

Glacier Gorge is another great example of the work of glaciers, and is perhaps more typical. It is well-rounded on the bottom, headed by a great cirque, or semicircular cliffs forming a headwall, contains several lakes, and leads out toward Bierstadt Moraine where much of the glacial debris was deposited. Starting at the head of Glacier Gorge, the following lakes may be seen: unnamed Iceland and Italy are the first two small lakes recognizable by their shapes; below them is Green Lake,

The trough. Bulls-eye can be seen at middle right of picture.

Photo by — Lloyd O. Timblin Jr.

which is shaped like South America; Frozen Lake is partly hidden by the great Spear Head jutting out into Glacier Gorge from Chief's Head; Blue Lake is closer to Longs; Black Lake in the bottom of the Gorge; and Shelf Lake is a good example of a hanging valley across the Gorge; on down the valley is Jewel Lake and out just beyond it, the larger Lake Mills; part of Lake Haiyaha can been seen some distance beyond, but Dream Lake and Loch Vale cannot be seen; Nymph, Bear, and Bierstadt are the remaining lakes in that direction.

None of the Park glaciers may be seen from this point. An interesting story was told to the late Charles Hewes by a Mr. Holt of Chicago who related how he had received directions for climbing Longs Peak from Carlisle Lamb in the early days. These directions included the possibility of seeing Hallet's Glacier (now called Rowe Glacier) from the Keyhole. Mr. Holt and his party looked in vain for Hallet's Glacier and failed to see it, though the day was clear. When they returned, they told Carlisle, who drawled out, "Well I've never seen it myself, but I have pointed it out to a lot of folks and generally they could see it."

On days when the peak is closed in by fog and climbers feel that they are being gypped by the lack of a good view, a resourceful guide can easily point out Kansas City, Chicago, Lake Michigan, and the Golden Gate Bridge. At least the guide can point in their direction and also include any other requested features.

In order to save time on a real climb, the lakes in Wild Basin are usually pointed out as the party descends, but for this work, they will be named now. Far across to the left and on a well-timbered slope is Finch Lake. Nearest and most evident is Sand Beach Lake. To the right, with its far shore line in view, is Thunder Lake. Above and around the shoulder of Mt. Tanima is Eagle Lake. Beyond that and high up against the Continental Divide is Junco Lake. The rounded mountain just beyond is Mount Copeland. Pikes Peak, if the day is sufficiently clear, may be seen directly over the left-hand snow patch of two which persist on bald-topped Meadow Mountain farthest left.

Some other activities are popular on top. Everyone wants to sign the register which is kept in a sturdy plastic cylinder among the rocks of the topmost cairn. Most climbers wish to eat their delayed lunch, but if you do not feel well, you had better skip it. Anyone can benefit by a few minutes of looking and resting before eating, and if the day is mild, some will stretch out and relax after eating. Others take pictures or want their picture taken on the highest rock. We pack out all our trash, since there is no longer a trash can on the summit. One more final thing before the descent: we should look around to see that no one has left anything. It is a long way back from just a little way down. The party should start down before 1 p.m. unless the day is fair.

Many of the following photographs by Paul Nesbit have been taken from the original 1946 publication.

Longs Peak Trail Map

Illustrated by Paul Nesbit

LONGS PEAK TRAIL
West and South Sides

Summit · West Face · South Face · Home Stretch · The Notch · False Keyhole · Keyboard of the Winds · Keyhole 13,215' · Schist · Ledges or Shelf · Trough · Pagoda 13,491'

LONGS PEAK TRAIL

Mt. Meeker 13,911' · Longs Peak 14,255' · The Notch · Mt. Lady Washington 13,269' · North Face · Keyhole · Storm Peak 13,335' · East Face · Chasm View · Boulderfield · To Bear Lake · Glacial Cirques · Mills Glacier · (Behind Mt. Lady W.) (Leave horses) 12,000' · Chasm Lake Shelter Cabin · Columbine Falls · Springs · Granite Pass · Timberline · Peacock Lake · Snow · Jim's Grove · Timberline Cabin Site · U-Shaped glacial valley · 11,000' · Roaring Fork · Mills Moraine · Pine Ridge · Alpine Brook · To Storm Pass 0.7 mi. · 10,000' · Old Eugenia mine · Park Cars Here · Rocky Mt. Nat. Park Boundary · Inn Brook · Longs Peak Camp Grounds and Ranger Station 9,530' · Circle C Camp · Rocky Ridge Music Center · Salvation Army Camp "High Peak" · Old Hewes-Kirkwood Inn · J.J.K. Ranch · Beaver Ponds · Up N. · To Top Longs Peak 9 Miles or 6 Hours · Mrs. Ding's Cabin · © Paul Nesbit 1946 · To Allenspark 8 mi. So St. Vrain and Denver 73 mi. · Highway 7 Oiled · Covenant Heights Camp · Enos A. Mills Grove · Longs Peak Inn · To Estes Park 9 mi · Twin Sisters Trail 3.8 miles · To Cabin Rock

Life Zones	Continental	Dominant	Vegetation		Altitude	Barometer Reading	Boiling Point	Mean July	Temperatures
Alpine	(Arctic)	Alpine Flowers	Sedges		14,255 ft.	17.45 in.	185° F	52.0° F	20.3° F
Sub-Alpine	(Hudsonian)	Engelmann Spruce · Sub Alpine Fir · Limber Pine						Maximum	Minimum
Montane	(Canadian)	Lodgepole Pine · Quaking Aspen							
Sub-Montane	(Transition)	Ponderosa Pine · Douglas Fir			9,000 ft · 21.47 in. · 195° F · 69.4° F · 39.6° F				

Longs Peak over early
morning clouds.
Photo by — Paul Nesbit

Longs Peak and Glacier Gorge
from Dream Lake Trail.
Photo by — Paul Nesbit

Longs Peak from Deer Ridge
after a September snowstorm.
Photo by — Paul Nesbit

Mt. Meeker, Longs Peak, and
Mt. Lady Washington
(left to right) are seen here over
the historic Longs Peak Inn,
which burned June 9, 1949.
Photo by — Paul Nesbit

Wind-blown banner trees at timberline beside the trail.
Photo by — Paul Nesbit

Yellow-bellied Marmot or Woodchuck, on the very summit of Longs Peak.
Photo by — Paul Nesbit

Alpine forms of Buckwheat, Sunflower, Phlox, Clover, Sandwort, Pin, Saxifrage, Parry Primrose, Lily, Buttercup, Whitlow and Wallflower.
Photo by– Don Obee

White-tailed Ptarmigan on a September snow.
Photo by — Paul Nesbit

Approaching Longs Peak from
Mills Moraine.

Photo by — Paul Nesbit

Climbing below the Cable. Mills
Moraine and Tahosa
Valley in the distance
(old Cable Route).

Photo by — Paul Nesbit

Boulderfield and the North Face
of Longs Peak. The Keyhole is at
the extreme right.

Photo by — Paul Nesbit

The Keyhole and Agnes Vaille
Memorial Shelter Cabin.

Photo by — Paul Nesbit

The North Face over Boulderfield
Stable, no longer standing
(Cable Route shown).
Photo by — Paul Nesbit

Chasm View and the foot of the
cables. The climbing route is
marked (cables since removed).
Photo by — Paul Nesbit

The East Face and Broadway from
Chasm View. At far right, above
center, is the Ramp.
Photo by — Paul Nesbit

Crossing Snowbank
below the cables.
Photo by — Paul Nesbit

False Keyhole, seen from the ledges.
Photo by — Stan Adamson

Looking northwest to the
Never Summer Mountains
from the North Face.
Photo by — Paul Nesbit

Chiefs Head, and the cirque which
heads Glacier Gorge,
seen from the summit.
Photo by — Paul Nesbi

Chasm Lake from the top in late
July, still containing an iceberg.
Photo by — Paul Nesbit

Party descending the Homestretch.
Photo by — Paul Nesbit

An August storm,
seen from the Narrows.
Photo by — Stan Adamson

In the Trough.
Photo by — Stan Adamson

Norman Nesbit, buffeted by the
fierce winds at the Keyhole.
Photo by — Stan Adamson

The Ledges, Dec. 29, 1989.
Photo by — Carroll Clark

East Face of Longs Peak showing Classic Climbing Routes

Modified from charts by Gerald Clarke and Warren Gorrell, Jr., with additional information supplied by many climbers.

Points of Interest:

Ca Cables
Co The Corner
CV Chasm View
G   Glacier Ridge
L   Lamb's Slide
Nt Notch Chimneys
S   Staircase
T   Table Ledge

Climbing Routes:

A   Alexander's Chimney
BB Big Bear*
BC Broadway Cutoff
BT Big Toe
C   Cable Route
CC Chasm Cutoff
CD Crack of Delight
Ch Chasm Chimney

Cr Craig's Crack
DD Diagonal Direct
Di Diagonal
Dt Directissima
Du Dunn
D1 Diamond 1
D7 D-7
E   Eighth Route

Ec Eclipse
FC Fields Chimney
GA Glendennings Arete
GP Gray Pillar
GT Grand Traverse
H   Hornsby's Direct
HC Hornbein Crack
Hy Hypoteneuse

Additional routes on the Diamond and Alexanders Chimney areas shown on page 35.
Additional routes in the Chasm View area and Mt. Meeker shown on page 37.

NOTE: *Routes circa 1972. For free-climbing routes, see Roger Briggs, "Longs Peak Free Climbs," Rock and Ice Magazine, March/April 1986, and Clay Wadman in the Bibliography*

Points of Interest:

IW	Invisible Wall		
J	Jack of Diamonds		
JS	Joe's Solo		
K	Kiener's		
KD	Kor's Door		
LN	Little Notch		
NC	Notch Couloir		

Climbing Routes:

NN	Near North*	SS	Shining Slab	W3	Waterhole Number 3
No	North Chimney	St	Stepladder	Y	Yellow Wall
O	Obelisk*	SW	Striped Wall	ZB	Zumie's Buttress
OD	Overhanging Dihedral	TR	Thumb Route	ZC	Zumie's Couloir
RF	Right Fields	W	Window Route	ZZ	Zig Zags
SC	Schobinger's Cracks	WD	Window Direct		
SL	Stettner's Ledges	We	Weedings		

*an unfinished route. The two dashed lines are the easiest routes on the North Face and East Face. Arrows show where routes are hidden behind ridges. The larger dots were overnight bivouacs.

Views From The Summit

Looking northwest.
Over Shelf Lake is Thatchtop
Mountain, Flatttop Mountain
and the Never Summer Range.
Photo by — Paul Nesbit

Looking south.
Arapaho Peaks are in the center.
To the left is Mt. Evans. Above
the woman are Grays and
Torreys Peaks in the distance.
Photo by — Paul Nesbit

Never Summer Mountains
showing between thunderstorms.
Sun shining on the summit.
Photo by — Paul Nesbit

Looking south where Wild Basin
is filled with clouds.
Photo by — Paul Nesbit

Morning after a bivouac.
No place for a hangover.
Photo by — Dale Johnson

Looking straight down past foot
in stirrup to Roskosz, Broadway, and
Mills Glacier (*not sky*).
Photo by — Layton Kor

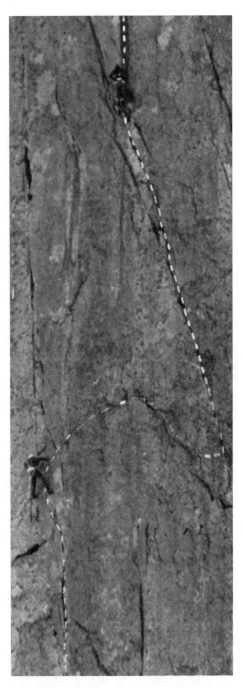

Telephoto from Mount Lady Washington
of Kor (above) belaying Roskosz (below)
on the Yellow Wall. Route is marked.
Photo by — John A. Kimmel

Ray Northcutt
leading his Diagonal Route.
Photo by — Layton Kor

Longs Peak seen rising 2,470 feet
above Chasm Lake.
Photo by — Paul Nesbit

Billy Westbay on the Diamond.
Photo by — Jim Detterline

The narrowest place on Broadway.
Routes to Chasm View marked:
Hornbein's on the left,
Carter's on the right.
Photo by — Norman Nesbit

Routes on Diamond area of East Face:
W Window, Hy Hypoteneuse, O Obelisk,
Cu Curving Vine, DM D Minor 7, D7 D-7,
BD Black Dagger, F Forrest's Finish, Y Yellow Wall,
D1 Diamond 1 or Ace of Diamonds,
J Jack of Diamonds, EM Enos Mills Wall, Du Dunn.
Photo by — Paul Nesbit

Looking down as two climbers
"top out" from Cable on August 1,
1965, in 8 inches of fresh snow.

Larry Dalke leading the third pitch
of Gray Pillar.
Photo by — Dalke & Goss

Details of Alexanders Chimney (AC) area.
AT Alexanders Traverse, B Bongalong,
D Kors Door, GA Glendenning's Arete,
K Kuncl Direct, LD Left Detour, R Right Detour,
TP Fricke's Trash Patrol.

Some of Kor's equipment
carried on the
Yellow Wall of the Diamond.

1 Stirrup, 2 Bong bongs, 3 Rope,
4 Pitons, 5 "Rurps" 6 Angles,
7 Carabiners, 8 Drill, 9 Hangers,
10 Bolts, 11 Light rope, 12 Sling,
13 Piton hammers.

1 Down jacket, 2 Pack, 3 Sweater,
4 Shoes, 5 Stocking cap, 6 Parka,
7 & 7 Food, 8 Stockings,
9 Knickers.

A rack of climbing equipment
for the Diamond, circa 1989,
used by Roger Briggs.
Photo by — Stan Adamson

A modern day technical
climber on Longs.
Photo by — Jim Detterline

Bob Boucher using Aid (4) on the Grand Traverse on the Diamond.
Photo by — *Pat Ament*

Tin plate left on Longs Peak by G.T. Dell, S. Williams and W.M. LaShell on Sept. 1, 1877. Found among rocks a little way down the east side by Dale Johnson, nearly 86 years later, Aug. 24, 1963.

Chasm Wall from Chasm View (CV) toward Mt. Lady Washington. Routes from left to right below Broadway and Chasm Cut-off: North Chimney, Eclipse, Zig Zags, Invisible Wall, Red Wall, Directissima, Indirectissima, Van Diver's Fantasy, Fisherman's Fantasy, Fifth Avenue, 42nd Street, Rollyco Stair (lower right, not shown).

North Face of Mt. Meeker. Ships Prow in lower right. Routes from left to right: Hiker's route to summit, Concave, Cobra, Swayback, East Arete, Flying Buttress, Stromboli, Portal and Gangplank. Nose of Ships Prow, Nexus Corner, & Step One not shown.

The Narrows.

Photo by — Brian Lewis

The Descent

The point of descent is marked with an arrow on a cairn. It leads off about straight south from the high point. The first section is the Home Stretch. The route descends over slanting slabs of granite with numerous cracks and crevices. With good footwear, experienced persons may walk down without using their hands. However, most prefer to sit out this stretch. That is, they use their five-wheel brakes, the seat being the fifth and most widely used in more ways than one. Before long, such persons may tie a sweater around their waist so that it will hang down and hide the see-through spot, or else they want to hang behind everyone else, or perhaps they will submit to a duct tape patch. Anyway, the safest way is to face outward and use a hand behind, or the seat, when the need is felt. Your feet are less likely to slip when you walk if you lean forward as you descend with your knees bent, thus throwing your weight more perpendicularly to the rocks and securing more traction.

At the foot of the Home Stretch the route turns toward the right and traverses the Narrows. One of the dangers of climbing without a guide is the possibility that thick clouds may settle over the Peak and obscure all but a few feet of the route ahead, However, this danger is minimized by the fact that every fifty feet or so, depending upon the terrain, there are colored bulls-eyes about six inches across painted upon the rocks to show the route. These have yellow centers with red borders. You should not proceed along what you think is the way, unless you see one of these markers ahead. They mark the route between the top and the Keyhole, and are not found elsewhere.

The Narrows look worse than they are. At places several may stroll abreast. At the narrower places there are good hand holds, but you may walk without using them. Over the edge is not a very high drop, although is quite perpendicular. If you get nervous, you may turn your attention to the lichens growing on the rock wall beside you. There are several kinds and shades of color.

The formation of the Narrows was evidently caused by a great fault or slip of one part of the mountain in relation to the other part, perhaps even before it was a mountain.

Around the corner we start down the long Trough. If there is much snow, keep farther to the right which means that you will have more of the slanting bare rock, especially near the top. For the most part, the Trough contains a great deal of loose rock and gravel, but it is not steep enough for rolling rocks to gain great momentum. However, it is well to watch your footing and not disturb the loose ones, nor allow your ankle to be turned by one. If an ankle starts to turn, go limp. The danger of a rock rolling on another member of the party can be greatly checked by the standard method of zigzagging back and forth in such a way that the climbers are not usually directly above or below one another. Beware of stepping on a rock where it is covered by a little gravel. Your foot may slide surprisingly.

About a third of the way down and toward the right are some large light-colored blocks containing a poor grade of garnets as dark circular masses up to two inches in diameter. Remember it is forbidden to take specimens in a National Park. Leave them for others to enjoy.

The Trough continues on down to the bottom of Glacier Gorge, but do not descend below the stone monument which is less than halfway down, where the trail leaves the Trough and goes to the right along the Ledges or Shelf to the Keyhole. The route follows a break in the rocks at the foot of the steeper cliffs. An unpleasantness lies in the fact that in order to get past some smooth and steeply inclined "boiler scale" rocks, we must climb upward a hundred feet or so and then back down. The way has its attractiveness, however. It lies along another fault plane which clearly shows *slickenside*, or rocks which have been smoothed or polished by the movement of rock against rock along the cracks under great pressure. Furthermore, this is the most likely place along the way to find Sky Pilots, a blue alpine polemonium flower, and the deep pink Parry Primrose. Both of these are among the most showy alpine flowers, but neither has a pleasant fragrance. Do not under any circumstances pick these flowers. The fact that they are there at all is evidence of the fact that thousands have restrained such tendencies.

At the top of this ascent, one may be inclined to continue on up the slope to the ridge. This leads to the place known as the False Keyhole. It is also called the Transom and can be negotiated along a narrow and high ledge from which there has been one fatal fall. So instead of crawling through the Transom, it is better to watch the trail signs, avoid the extra climb, and return through the real Keyhole. On this route there is a place where a couple of steel spikes have been placed and wisely so. It does not seem dangerous because the rocks are not so steep, but if you did accidently lose balance or slip, you would have a hard time stopping on the smooth rocks below. Accidents are liable to happen when you are fatigued. About 150 feet before you reach the Keyhole, you may notice a rock just to the right of the trail which contains black, coal-like crystals of tourmaline.

The Keyhole is a good place for an eye-full when going either way. It is also a place for a frequent ear-full of wind. Take your last look at Glacier Gorge and scoot down some smooth rocks. Then you will suddenly be aware of a beehive-shaped stone structure to your right. It is the Keyhole Shelter Cabin or "Agnes Vaille Memorial Shelter." The water, sand, cement, and window and door parts were all laboriously carried by a man from the end of the horse trail in Boulderfield. He commonly carried eighty pounds to the load and made six trips a day.

Agnes Vaille Tragedy

To the left of the shelter door, the inscription on a bronze tablet reads: "Agnes Wolcott Vaille. This shelter commemorates a Colorado mountaineer conquered by winter after scaling the precipice, Jan. 12, 1925, and one who lost his life in an effort to aid her, Herbert Sortland."[5]

Agnes Vaille, on her fourth attempt, and in spite of dissuasion, realized her ambition to climb the East Face in winter time, but due to temporary physical condition and after 25 hours of steady climbing from timberline, did not have the reserve necessary to again reach shelter in the face of below zero weather and stormy conditions. Her Swiss companion, Walter Kiener, left her and managed to reach Timberline Cabin where he met a search party. With great effort, Kiener and only one of the rescuers, Jacob Christen, were able to reach Miss Vaille, but too late. She died from exhaustion and freezing some

200 feet down the talus slope below the rocks on the North Face and not here at the Keyhole.

Herbert Sortland was a member of the rescue party who had to turn back, but never quite reached safety. It was six weeks before his body was found a short distance beyond Longs Peak Inn where he had been employed as a caretaker. He had lost his way in the storm and suffered a broken hip.

Mr. Kiener was hospitalized and lost all but one of his fingertips, all of his toes and part of the left foot due to freezing. Thus impaired for his former occupation, he started to college, worked his way to a Doctor's degree in botany, and worked with the Game, Forestation, and Parks Commission of the state of Nebraska. For several succeeding summers Kiener was a fire lookout on Twin Sisters Mountain. Guiding on Longs Peak then became for a time a means to support his research work on the vegetation of the Peak, chiefly of the tundra zone above timberline. In connection therewith, he

Agnes Vaille Shelter.
Photo by — Lloyd O. Timblin Jr.

[5]The first time Paul Nesbit climbed Longs Peak, it was also Herbert Sortland's first climb.

maintained a thermograph station on Broadway above Alexander's Chimney, and made many climbs that far on the East Face to attend to it. The writer well remembers how Walter made his first climb up Longs Peak after the tragedy. He accompanied our party to Boulderfield and left us to climb the North Face before the cables were in place. When we reached the top, he was already there. His knees and elbows were wet and worn, but he was much elated that he could still climb mountains. He signed the register, "With cut wings coming over the North Face."

Homeward Bound

From the Keyhole, the old Boulderfield Shelter site may possibly be seen in the approximate center of the rocky expanse of Boulderfield. Good climbers can make it from the Keyhole to the shelter site in five minutes. On the other hand, it may take over an hour for some who are nearly exhausted and whose leg muscles no longer support them steadily. In case there are horses waiting at the shelter to be mounted, someone should go ahead to ready them and thus save several minutes. Those who have camped in one of the back country sites at Boulderfield can rest again sooner than most.

The ride or hike homeward for a tired party is frequently a plodding affair. Thoughts of the comparative comforts at the foot of the trail, of the time and distance to be covered, of the evening meal, of concern due to threatening clouds, or wishes that the rain would cease, all mingle with thoughts of the day's great experiences and accomplishments. Many are so tired that they do not glance back at the monarch they have surmounted unless it is suggested. Yet what a feeling of exultation it can be to say to oneself, "I've climbed to the very summit of that old peak. I was up there where I could look down on every one of these other imposing mountains. No one can ever take that experience away from me."

The Great East Face

The great East Face with its 1,675 feet of nearly perpendicular drop and its variety of difficult climbs commands the respect of any climber. The stories of the perilous descents of Lamb and Mills, long before others dared to attempt the ascent, enhanced the awe with which it was long regarded. For more than fifty years it was a precipice to be avoided.

Then in 1922, Professor J. W. Alexander of Princeton University literally broke the ice when he made a solo ascent using Lambs Slide. The climb had been planned with Ranger Jack Moomaw, but Jack was unable to go on that day. The two did climb again and take pictures just two days later, this time using the chimney and traverse later named for Alexander.

When the time has come for a human step forward, there may be more than one with the same idea. Thus pioneering credit is also due Dudley Smith of Denver, who after two years of study had sketched almost the same ascent and

The East Face.

Photo by — Lloyd O. Timblin Jr.

41

discussed it with Carl Blaurock and John Hart. They were astounded to read in the newspaper that Alexander had climbed this route, but they proceeded to climb as planned, and just three days later. They were joined by Mr. and Mrs. Herman Buhl, Frank Shirmer and Herbert Wortman. Their ascent is described in *Trail and Timberline* of December, 1923, by Blaurock They "had come prepared with two ice axes and 75 feet of alpine rope."

It has taken many climbers with adventurous spirits to pioneer the ways since 1864 when W.N. Byers, founder of the *Rocky Mountain News*, failed in an extended attempt to climb Longs Peak and predicted (as Pike never did concerning Pikes Peak) that no man would reach its summit, although he conceded a bare possibility.

Since 1868, when Byers himself was a member of the party which first stood on the top of Longs Peak, crevice grapplers have been continually discovering that routes existed where none had been supposed. At first it took only exploratory efforts to learn that when one sought a route it could often be found. Later the developments of climbing techniques and equipment have greatly accelerated the accomplishments of climbers and more and more difficult routes have been found.

Introducing the Diamond

Just as the whole East Face was for so long regarded as insurmountable, so for several more years the cliff climbers skirted its sheerest portion and regarded it as out of their world. Then, just as details of the whole East Face had earlier been studied with a view of climbing it, so some began to study the large, highest, unclimbed section, the most smoothly vertical part directly beneath the summit, and above Broadway. As interest increased, it came to be called the Diamond. It is roughly that shape, although its corners have been cut, thus increasing the facets and making it roughly octagonal in a vertical plane.

The Diamond.

Photo by — Lloyd O. Timblin Jr.

There it has stood, a diamond in the rough, as it was first exposed and cut by the plucking action of a glacier during the ice age; rough enough and with flaws enough to make climbing possible when the time was right. There it stands today, proudly displayed in its rock-bound setting, highest on the most showy flank where it is best seen from the haunts of men; there on the most fascinating peak of the southern Rockies.

A diamond is the hardest natural substance known and it has also been long regarded as a symbol of ultimate attainments, as in marriage and in value. This Diamond, to a cliff hanger's eye, as a diamond to a maiden's, would be a crowning glory. Only an expert climber would consider this one in any way attainable, yet there it was, a virgin wall to be wooed and won by him who could demonstrate superior prowess. Thus the Diamond came to symbolize the hardest climb on the mountain and displayed it provokingly. It was the mountain's dare.

How Do They Climb?

How could anyone really hope to meet such a dare? What have been the developments in the art of rock climbing that have made such climbs thinkable? "I don't see how they do it!" is a common exclamation, even concerning less spectacular climbs. That is not easy to explain. As well, try to tell how one composes a symphony, paints a masterpiece, writes a classic, or invents a computer. Only a smattering will be told in order to provide an introduction to rock climbing for the general reader, explain some of the special terms commonly used, and establish a realistic setting for the Diamond story.

The Diamond and most other strenuous routes are not smooth unbroken rock. At times there will be projections for hand holds. As in life, the bumps are what you climb on if you learn to take advantage of them. There are also cracks of various widths and lengths. Some are vertical and wide enough to put an arm or foot in, and by wedging pressure to both sides, *jamming*, you may hold tight or work your way upward. Other vertical cracks are wide enough to enter and then are called *chimneys*. In these one may inch upward by pressing against opposite sides. Sometimes rocks or boulders fall into chimneys and become wedged, thus tending to block the passageway. These are called *chockstones*. They, and other types of *overhangs* or roofs where the rock juts out over your head, present greater difficulties where you may have to perform strenuous acrobatics over space as you climb out under, and raise yourself over such an edge, grappling for scanty hand holds.

At places you may need to make a *traverse*, that is to cross to right or left. Then you will choose ledges if they are available. If a foot wide, you can easily walk one. If an inch or less, there may still be some footing to walk on, if the cliff slants away enough for you to maintain your balance, and if you have the nerve. A large supply of the latter may make hard-looking places easy. Why creep and crawl if you can stand and walk? Why take time to inch along and search for hand holds if you can calmly step across? Self-confidence and balance can save hours of precious time. If you can confidently walk on scanty footholds six feet high, you can, by much practice and experience, learn to do it safely 600 feet high. How? How do people build skyscrapers? How do they learn to perform on a flying trapeze? If a person wants badly enough to do something, he or she can do wonders. We tend to forget it because we live such easy, sheltered lives. If you can, with aids, master the technique of climbing twenty feet up a crack, you can climb 1,000 feet. The twenty feet is commonplace; the 1,000 feet spectacular. It requires great nerve. If you do not have it, you must either develop it, or decide that the top climbs are not for you.

But fortunately climbing has been made easier and safer than described so far. *Pitons*, metal spikes that could be driven into cracks, offered early roped climbers protection in case of a fall. Driven in with a piton hammer carried for the purpose, some pitons are thicker or longer than others. Some are flattened horizontally, some vertically. Some are angled for cracks of different widths. Some are short, thin knife blades for very narrow cracks. Each has an eye-hole or ring just beneath the head through which the climber's rope can be strung.

In the era when climbing began on the Diamond (the 1960s) it was done as follows:

When you drove a proper piton into a crack, you could tell by the sound of "ping" when it was safely tight, and you could test it. Next you snapped through the eye of the piton an oval-shaped snap-link called a *carabiner*. This has a gate on one side which can be opened by pressing in as with a safety pin, but it is not a pin and is much more stoutly made. Also, through the gate of a carabiner may easily be snapped a climbing rope at any position along its length. Then a climber with an end of a rope securely fastened at the waist may easily snap it into and out of a carabiner, and also let it run through several of them. Thus the climber is secured to the rocks by a rope and hands and body are given freedom of movement as desired.

This freedom for a climber to move ahead, and yet for any fall to be quickly checked, was provided by a climbing partner either ahead or behind. This other essential member, at any dangerous or difficult time, would have selected the best available stance and been secured tightly to a piton if need be. This *anchor man* then *belayed* the moving climber by playing out just the needed amount of rope to allow for necessary movement and to provide a safeguard in case of a fall.

The one who climbed ahead or *led* had the more difficult and dangerous role. The leader not only climbed, but had to place the needed pitons at proper intervals during ascent. If natural holds on the rock were inadequate or too risky, the leader may have placed some pitons as *direct aid*, that is as hand holds, or to stand on, or to hang from. This last may be by means of *stirrups* or *slings* to hang from the attached carabiner and then to stand in. In addition a leader may resort to *tension climbing*, whereby a signal is given by the leader to the belayer to hold the leader tight to a nearly vertical wall and thus free his hands. When you use such direct aids, it is called *artificial climbing*.

Placing pitons was a time-consuming process and was less needed when the leader could use natural hand and footholds and ascend by *free climbing*, that is by balance and without direct aid. However, when free climbing was done in any *exposed* place, that is, where the slope was so steep that an unexpected slip could mean a dangerous fall, the leader placed pitons at frequent intervals and snapped the climbing rope through the series of carabiners. When the climber lost balance on even a moderate slope, he or she could tumble over and over and never regain control, except for the rope in the hands of a skilled belayer. If one climbed six feet above the last piton and fell, they would drop six feet below that piton, or a distance of twelve feet before the rope would naturally begin to check the fall. An expert belayer could do a great deal to gradually stop this by providing a *dynamic belay*. This greatly reduces the effect of a sudden jerk, which if severe, would be more liable to pull out a piton, break the carabiner or rope, injure the fallen climber's body, or pull the belayer from a secure position. This last must never happen. However, if a leader was making a traverse and fell, he or she would pendulum down beneath the last piton, but the distance and consequences for the same distance beyond the piton might be less than half as severe.

When the leader had climbed a suitable distance, often to the first good stance beyond a difficult or tricky stretch, the leader would in turn assume a belaying position, often anchoring tightly to a piton, bracing as best as possible, passing the rope around his or her body and then holding it by a hand before and the other after, in order to feel, take in, let out, brake, and control the movement of the rope.

While thus belayed the second person climbed, removing the "hardware" and bringing it along. Thus the pitons could be used again at higher points. This saved expense, left the rock clean for any who followed to practice their own techniques, and reduced the weight that they had to carry.

Three-person teams were also common and introduced both advantages and disadvantages.

From one such belay point to the next is called a *pitch* or a *lead*. If one climber were more experienced, he or she might lead all of the pitches. If they were more equally qualified, they usually took turns leading. Obviously, the second person who was belayed from above would be checked almost as soon as a fall occurred and was thus in less danger.

In places, adequate cracks for pitons might be lacking, or extra safety desired for a more crucial anchor point. For such cases a small rock drill was carried, a small hole drilled into the solid rock and short *expansion bolts* inserted and tightened. These were generally left in place and not removed.

To descend might have been easy if one *rappelled* backward down a hanging rope, controlling the rate of descent by means of the friction applied as the rope was properly placed about the body and/or through a carabiner attached to a body sling. If one did not wish to go back up, the rope was doubled and then could be pulled down by pulling on one end. If one wished to resume the climb another day, *fixed rope* would be left securely attached to pitons or to a bolt. Then one might later *prusik* or *jumar* back up to the former position. This was accomplished by using three loops of light rope, each tied or attached to the fixed rope by a *prusik knot* or *jumar ascender*. Each such knot or jumar and its attached loop could be slid up the climbing rope when there was no weight upon it, but held tight at that position whenever there was the downward pull of a person's weight.

One of the three slings was passed about the climber's chest, and a foot placed in each of the others. By standing in one loop, the others bore no weight and could be moved upward. Then one stepped up into the position of the higher loop and repeated the process. The body sling provided an extra factor of safety and left both hands free to move up the knots or jumars.

Climbing technique and philosophy have changed dramatically since the Diamond was first conquered. Along with the general growth of environmental concerns, today's climbers attempt to leave as few signs of their passing as possible, and so have developed clean-climbing techniques which involve far fewer aids than in the past. Most of the routes originally climbed with the heavy equipment of the past have now been free-climbed. Nuts, artificial chockstones, and mechanical camming devices have enabled today's climbers not only to climb more cleanly, but also to climb routes inaccessible before. Where before climbing could be engaged in by any relatively fit person willing to learn a few fairly simple techniques and take some spectacular, calculated risks, today's techniques are a quantum leap forward, elevating climbing to a highly sophisticated athletic art form. To learn more about today's techniques, one might read *How to Rock Climb* by John Long (Globe Pequot, Guilford, CT, 2002). But this sport cannot be learned from a book. Lessons and practice are the only way to go.

It should be obvious that this brief description merely introduces the elementary practices that THEY use in rock climbing. It is entirely inadequate for telling YOU how to climb. In order to safely learn how to climb, you must do a great deal of practicing, and much of that with experts. You should practice, practice, practice tying the needed knots, handling ropes and keeping them untangled and placing of hardware in various types of cracks and from every position, for your life will depend upon them. You need to develop arm and hand muscles, skills of balance, of jamming, of using hand holds of various kinds and heights in various positions, of belaying from many types of stances, and of holding actual practice falls. You need the experience when you are well-belayed in order to better handle yourself and to learn just what is the margin of safety so that you may remain within it. No would-be tightrope walker would start practicing fifty feet high after merely reading how to do it. Climbers need an even greater variety of skills, but many of them are less evident and they should be developed in safer places.

Fortunately the aspiring cloud pusher can in these days find others to climb with and you may also attend one of the many climbing schools which are held by the various active mountain clubs around the country. And more fortunately for the summer visitor to the Longs Peak area, there is usually a guide service available under concession permit of the National Park Service. They have classes and equipment for beginning, intermediate, and advanced climbing pupils in addition to their guided trips up various Longs Peak routes. The extra feeling of confidence with a group, if inspired by expert leadership, can add much to your enjoyment and accomplishments.

An important, but often hidden factor, and at times as crucial as technical know-how, is your physical condition. Fortunately, it too is acquired from practice climbs. You should always have the physical reserve which adds both to the feeling of wellbeing and to safety. It is of little value to know what to do, but to be so exhausted as to become careless or lacking in coordination. In order to overcome the uneasiness created by severe exposure, you need superb self-confidence, and much of that may come from a positive feeling of being physically fit. On the other hand, any lack of that feeling, even though subconscious, can affect your mental attitude and cause trouble at times of great stress.

All of the above situations are made increasingly difficult by the high altitude of the rock climbs on Longs Peak and the resultant more severe strain upon one's energies, and yet not severe enough to keep most from trying. Rocks may be wet either from small watercourses, from melting snows, or from frequent thunderstorms. Preceding these storms there may be gusty winds to throw one off balance. Early morning may find *verglas*, a coating of ice over the rocks where water has run on a cold night. If a storm comes up when you are climbing a stern, cold wall, you must retreat, continue to climb, or wait. You must always strike a balance between progress and fleeting time. You cannot be as safe when time has exhausted your physical resources, or numbed you with cold, or brought on darkness. Fatigue is a prime cause of accidents and may take its toll after the climax of the most difficult pitches are past.

An expert climber will become adept at taking all of the above factors into account and many others, including all members of the climbing party. Great experience may induce confidence. Climbers must be fearless but not foolish. They should tend toward caution and avoid risk and recklessness. They will strive to maintain a margin of safety. They will continually be thinking ahead and that will include checking equipment both as to its condition and adequacy. They will study the route with care, taking into account the nature and firmness of the rocks, and the likelihood of rocks falling from above and the courses they will take. Rocks are more liable to fall during a storm or when a warm sun melts ice which may have held rocks in place. In falling from a height, stones may attain the speed of bullets, and small ones be as hard to see and as dangerous. A safety helmet is essential—especially for an anchor man who remains directly below a climber, and also in case of a fall. They have little leeway for dodging rocks which might become dislodged.

Over the years the knowledge and practice of better climbing techniques has greatly improved. This may be illustrated by comparing one later with two former accidents.

In 1926 two climbers with no rope were starting up the Chimneys above Broadway. The sub-headline on the next day's newspaper tells the story: "Companion hears Forrest Ketring's cry of terror and, powerless to help, sees body flash past him on a precipice and hurtle to depths below."

In 1929, we read the following parts of a newspaper account of another accident at the same locality (quotations from *The Rocky Mountain News.*):

> "I was holding the lower end of a 30 yard rope and my friend (above) had succeeded in fastening it, rather insecurely, to a crag, when I saw him slip," Stacher said. "Don't go up there, it's not safe," Stacher had warned Thiemeyer.
>
> "Oh, I can make it all right," answered Thiemeyer, who was a native of Switzerland, and had often remarked that there were no mountains in Colorado worth climbing. A moment later he fell.

The attitude expressed in the last paragraph of recklessness and audacity is certainly conducive to accidents. Habitual respect of the forces of nature is an important part of safety. Without digressing further on attitudes, the following is given in order that the climbing techniques involved may be compared with those above. It was written by Ranger Ernest K. Field and was printed in *Trail and Timberline*, December, 1948, under the heading, "An Accident on Longs Peak."

> At about noon on July 17 last summer, Bill Eubank and Brad Van Diver of Boulder had practically finished an uneventful climb of Stettner's Ledges on the East Face of Longs Peak. Van Diver was leading the last pitch and Eubank was belaying. When Van Diver was only a few feet from Broadway, he either slipped, or was struck in the head and momentarily stunned by a small rock falling from higher on the peak. In any event he fell about 40 feet as he was climbing some 20 feet above his last piton.
>
> Eubank fortunately was in an excellent belaying position and was anchored to his position by another piton. As Van Diver fell, Eubank was able to take in a small amount of stack and release sufficient rope to effect a dynamic belay when Van Diver reached the limit of his fall. While Eubank was lifted from his feet by the impact, he

was not pulled from the wall since he was held in by his anchor. Van Diver suffered a severe scalp laceration when he scraped his head against the wall as he felt, and was unconscious for three hours while Eubank rendered first aid and signaled for help.

A rescue party, led by Seasonal Ranger George Hurt, arrived at the scene several hours later and was able to get the injured climber off the face before dark. Van Diver enjoyed a complete recovery even though the doctor "lost count" of the number of stitches required to close the lacerations in the climber's scalp.

Both of these young men are very good climbers, and have studied a number of technical manuals on the subject. It is believed that this accident, although painful for Van Diver, illustrates how a good knowledge of climbing techniques, and a proper application of the same, prevented a tragedy that could well have been fatal to both men. It is believed, however, that these young men will not again climb the excessive distance of 20 feet beyond their last piton.

It is hoped that ambitious climbers may learn the lesson illustrated by these three accidents and practice their techniques beforehand. It is too late to get out the manual and study it after a slip has occurred on the East Face. It should be further noted that Van Diver was rescued the same day, whereas the Stachers, in the second accident above, were marooned on the East Face all night, and rescued the following day. Had Thiemeyer only been injured, he might yet have died of shock and exposure. The prompt rescue at the later date was due to at least two factors. Eubank and Van Diver were wiser climbers in that they started earlier in the day, and the National Park Service is now better prepared to effect a quick rescue, especially when they are informed of the climb beforehand, as will be done by all good climbers attempting the more difficult routes.

The Diamond from Chasm Lake.

Photo by — Bob Mills

Engaging the Virgin Wall

Where there is the challenge of an unclimbed wall, there will in time appear those rare men or women who seek to meet it, who are eager to try new things, and who have taken great pains to develop the necessary skills. When a mountain's time has come, there will be several such individuals, and it might as well give up. To those who have mastered the needed skills, things may look possible which are beyond the ken of others.

Such a climber was Dale Johnson of Boulder, Colorado. After long study, he first laid actual plans with Bob Sutton to mount the Diamond. However, discussion with the local National Park

47

Service, which is required before attempting unusual climbs, revealed that they did not favor any attempt upon the Diamond. Thus the climbers discovered that, in addition to the natural difficulties imposed by the frigid, domineering wall, there were man-made hindrances to be surmounted. Such is commonly the case with those who dare to move ahead of the crowd. After one first decides "it can be done", and secondly, "I will do it," then the voice of public opinion or of authority often says, "It's unthinkable. You mustn't. It's too risky." Thus are the natural difficulties compounded; thus are many worthy projects stymied, and thus does mankind block or delay its own progress. However, thus is humanity also saved from many foolish adventures and waste of lives and resources. And in that way, the stage and the plot are set for many a fascinating story, both in fiction and in the history of mankind's struggles against odds and uncertainties, with the accompanying suspense and the doubtful final outcome. Let us now follow this real-life story of "Engaging the Virgin Wall" or "Polishing the Diamond" and see how it turned out.

Back in 1922, when Alexander wanted to try to climb the East Face, there were no evident restrictions. He was free to climb on his own responsibility. The risks, and the consequent penalties or honors were his and his alone. He succeeded, as responsible men and women often do. But over the intervening years, would-be climbers had done some foolish and tragic things. Not only had some lost their own lives, but the Park Rangers had many times been called upon to risk their lives in rescue work. Many long and expensive days had been spent in searching for, and in carrying out, the victims.

The superintendent of Rocky Mountain National Park is charged with the responsibility of managing the whole area and is given broad powers to do so. If some wish to risk their own lives, that is their business, but it becomes the superintendent's business when they get into trouble and their lives depend upon the assistance of the rangers. Suppose two climbers get stuck, or have an accident near the midpoint of a 1,000 foot, sheer precipice. Can anyone then refuse to try to save their lives? Hardly. Yet the climbers who reached an impasse were supposedly among the best. How wise is it then to send perhaps less able and reluctant rangers to risk their lives in the rescue? But suppose that the daring climbers succeed, as is likely. Then, might not the publicity given them attract other climbers, thus perpetuating the problems? Or, at some point, could increased climbing be liable to result in failure and disaster, which might have better been avoided, along with the public criticism which would have been aroused?

At the time Johnson was expected to make considerable use of drilled bolts. Some who opposed the climb made a point that this would result in defacement of the rocks, and there are regulations prohibiting this. The objection was publicized in the papers, but was later dropped. But Johnson had a rare determination to succeed, an important characteristic of climbers. The objections of the National Park Service to unnecessarily risking their rangers could be met by recruiting his own volunteer support party and enlarging his preparation for every conceivable emergency. Fortunately, the city of Boulder, where the University of Colorado is located, had long been a climbing center and there were excellent climbers available and willing to become members of a support and rescue party. In fact, there had been for some time organized there the Rocky Mountain Rescue Group which had many times demonstrated the value of their training and experience in rescue work. Here also were located two important establishments supplying the best in mountaineering equipment, Mountain Sports, Inc., and Holubar Mountaineering, Ltd. The decision in 1954 was to refuse Johnson permission to attempt the climb.

It seemed better to say, "No," beforehand because it could not be said later if their lives were "hanging by a thread." Anyway, the Diamond was regarded by all but a few climbers as just too nearly impossible.

Likewise an application by Dick Pownall, later to become a member of the 1963 American Mount Everest Expedition, and Bill Dunaway was turned down in 1955, even though they had lined up a well-equipped support party from among Fort Carson climbers. Johnson sounded out the local officials again in 1957 and found the door still closed. In 1958, now manager of Gerry Mountain Sports, he made a more complete and formal application including photographs, ability certificates, and detailed plans. This time Ray Northcutt was to be his climbing partner, and Layton Kor, whose name will appear again, and Albert Riordan were listed as alternates These requests followed a great deal more preparatory climbing on difficult Longs Peak routes and elsewhere. In June of 1958 the *Estes Park Trail* had editorialized in favor of giving permission for the climb.

But the local Park Service administration was still not inclined to grant the needed approval, although they had given the matter considerably more study, and discussions had been held with other officials including those from Grand Teton and Yosemite National Parks, two important parks for rock climbing.

When able people of determination find themselves thwarted, they are likely to try other ways, for "Where there's a will, there's a way." Hoping to strengthen their case and to convince the officials that the Diamond could be climbed, Ray Northcutt and George Lamb began in 1958 to work on the "Diagonal" route. This one had not attracted attention, and because it was between other routes below Broadway, it had not been declared "off limits."

The Diagonal climb proved to be no small undertaking. The original plan was to follow a crack which started at the base of the wall and ran diagonally upward and toward the left across some difficult overhangs. Two climbing days in 1958 had been shortened by "violent hail and electrical storms." In early 1959, Northcutt, now aided by Layton Kor of Boulder, reached the dark vertical streaks caused by continual running water and the resulting lichen growth. Here the crack was playing out and the water and slippery lichens caused added difficulties.

A traverse to the right was chosen as the easier way, but it too was tricky. At the time there were no hand holds and the ledges narrowed down in places to a quarter of an inch. Fortunately the rock was not vertical and they crossed by balanced climbing.

This route was pushed upward on five different days, the first four all being cut short by storms. On the final day, July 19, 1959, they continued on through the storm and reached Broadway after 13 hours of continuous climbing.[6]

Now, however, permission to climb the Diamond seemed harder to obtain than ever, for the problems had been enlarged and must now await policy decisions from Washington. In Yosemite, El Capitan, a similar but much higher "impossible" wall, had been climbed. There was much publicity, and an illustrated story of the climb was sold and published. The Park service feared that the climb might have been made as a stunt primarily for publicity purposes. This brought in the consideration of commercialization, another area in which control is exercised. Now the matter had become a question of policy for the entire National Park Service. Thus, in early 1959, Director Conrad L. Wirth issued a statement from Washington barring such "stunt and daring trick climbing" while new regulations were being prepared. Meanwhile, the challenge of the unclimbed Diamond was making it more famous and attracting the attention of climbers in other areas and even in foreign countries. There it displayed an opportunity: Acres of Diamond, eighteen of them.

Mounting the Diamond

More than a year passed and in the summer of 1960 the new policies had been formulated in favor of allowing such climbs when certain rigid requirements had been met. Thereupon, James V. Lloyd, the superintendent of Rocky Mountain National Park, sent out application blanks simultaneously to all parties who had previously made known their interest in climbing the Diamond.

[6]See Northcutt's article in *The American Alpine Journal*, 1960:1, pp. 129-30.

Dale Johnson set about preparing to submit his application and contacted Ray Northcutt, but the chance for which they had worked so hard and waited so long came at an inopportune time. They both had jobs and had not been able to climb enough at high altitudes to be in top physical condition. Northcutt was committed to his work in Montana and could not get away. Then Johnson learned that two climbers from California were preparing an application and were already recruiting a support party. He redoubled his efforts.

The Californians, Robert Kamps, an elementary school teacher from North Hollywood, and David Rearick, who had just received his doctorate in mathematics from Cal Tech, had been climbing much of the summer and were already in good physical condition. For three weeks they had been climbing locally and had made an inquiry about climbing the Diamond. They too received an application blank and they were at once able to turn their whole attention to meeting the requirements. Their rock-climbing abilities had already been recognized in California where they had passed rigid tests and qualified with the Sierra Club as rock-climbing leaders. In addition, they had successfully climbed the Diagonal. The determination necessary for the Diamond climb was immediately evident in the ways they set about lining up their primary and secondary support parties and securing telegraphic confirmations of their successful, difficult climbs in Yosemite, the Teton Mountains, and on Devils Tower. Finally, their equipment was laid out and checked over by the rangers.

Their application was approved on Thursday, July 27th, for an attempt during the month of August. They had another four days for final preparations before they could touch the Diamond. They knew that Johnson would apply and that there might be others. It might be a race, and they were determined to be first.

All readers of mountaineering history will remember the fascinating story of the first ascent of the Matterhorn, and how through the years it had been thought impossible. Then several attempts were made. Finally, in 1865, Edward Whymper and his party were organized from Zermatt, Switzerland, after he had already seen an Italian party start out from their side and realized that they "had clearly stolen a march" on him. Nevertheless, Whymper's party arrived at the top first and saw the Italian party only 1,250 feet below. The leader of that party, J. A. Carrel, had been first to believe that it could be climbed, and it was his lifetime ambition to accomplish it. In Whymper's own words, Carrel "most deserved to be first upon its summit"[7].

After making arrangements for the support party to follow and bring more equipment, Rearick, Bob and Mrs. Bonnie Kamps, and Jack Laughlin, a helpful supporting friend from Hollywood, moved up to Chasm Lake Shelter on Saturday. Would it be necessary for them to share this small hut with a competing party? They did not know, but at least they got there first. On Sunday, the 31st, the support party arrived from Boulder. It consisted of Charles Roskosz (watch for his name to appear again), Dean Moore, Charles Alexander, and Gary Cole. Members of the Alpine Rescue Team from Evergreen, Colorado, led by Gordon Stocker, were available on call as secondary support.

With the arrival of the primary support party came a steady drizzle, but work went forward on the installation of fixed ropes as hand lines up North Chimney in order to make it easier to carry the gear up to the base of the Diamond. Rain drove the climbers back to the shelter that night instead of staying on Broadway as planned. Monday, the first of August, when they could start their direct attack for which the precipice had for millennia been waiting, dawned cold and windy, but clear, and spirits were high. No competitors had yet arrived. The two principal climbers left their shelter early and climbed over the cold, wet rocks and nylon ropes to Broadway, trusting the support party to finish the wearisome task of lugging more gear that far and of preparing there a comfortable bivouac site.

Let us now quote from the climbers' matter-of-fact report which they prepared for Rocky Mountain National Park files, and get their own story. Such reports are supposed to be regular procedure. Permissions to use this, and the excerpts which follow, have been granted.

[7]*Scrambles Amongst the Alps,* by Edward Whymper

Climbers' Report of the First Ascent of the Diamond

By David F. Rearick and Robert F. Kamps

The purpose of this report is to provide the Park and future climbing parties with technical information gained during the first ascent.

The actual climbing began at 9:30 a.m. on August 1. The first pitch, 140 feet, is easy free climbing. The second pitch is moderate to difficult face climbing on solid rock, leading to an overhang slanting to the right. The third pitch involves direct aid to ascend the right edge of this overhang, and ends on a grass-covered platform with a large (loose) boulder, easily visible from Chasm View. The fourth pitch starts up the inside of the corner above, gaining 30 feet by difficult free climbing until direct aid is necessary. Easy "nailing" brings one up to the conspicuous six-foot overhang above, and it was passed with a single piton. Increasingly difficult nailing is encountered in the wide grass-filled crack leading from here up to the Ramp. On the first ascent this section was being drenched by water falling free from the chimney near the top of the Diamond. The highest point reached August 1 was about 80 feet below the Ramp. A bolt was placed to reinforce the poor belay stance and to serve as a rappel anchor for the return to Broadway. The time of descent was 4:00 p.m., the early retreat being due to threatening weather.

On August 2 we prusiked back up and continued to the Ramp. This feature is a sloping shelf 6 to 8 feet wide and eminently unsuited for a bivouac site. Twenty feet higher, however, we discovered a good ledge on which a bivouac is possible. At the Ramp the nature of the rock takes a change for the worse, becoming rather loose and fractured. The wall leans outward constantly for the next 400 feet and we were climbing behind the falling water. The sixth pitch ascends the central crack system to a point about 115 feet above the Ramp. It is almost all direct aid, and piton placing is moderately difficult. Our second bolt was placed to anchor a belay in slings at the end of this pitch.

The seventh pitch continues straight up to a ledge about 225 feet above the Ramp. It is mostly moderately difficult to difficult direct aid climbing, except for the last 20 feet where the crack becomes suitable for jamming. The ledge is 2 feet wide and 7 feet long. We placed a third bolt here and pulled up the pack with our bivouac gear from its resting place on the ramp. It did not touch rock once on the way up.

Before dark the 8th pitch had been completed, to a point 100 feet above the ledge. It involves difficult nailing up a series of blocks and overhangs. A 4th bolt was placed at the top, and the leader descended to the ledge, removing the pitons on the way down.

We spent the night of August 2 on this two-foot ledge. The temperature was probably about 40 degrees, and our down jackets kept us comfortable. Early on August 3 the first man prusiked up the rope (dangling out from the rock) to the high point reached the previous evening, and continued on 30 feet to the point where the central chimney crosses the prominent transverse crack running across the Diamond. There is a good belay stance here in a small cave. The other climber followed on through and started nailing up the chimney. Water, moss, and overhanging chockstones soon forced a detour to a crack system a few feet to the left. At the end of this, the 9th pitch, a belay in slings was set up. At this point the wall finally ceases to be overhanging and becomes harder and the pitons more reliable.

The 10th pitch, about 60 feet long, finally brought us to a point at which we could re-enter the chimney, and the 11th and final pitch is free climbing up the chimney to the top. There were several huge blocks of ice in the chimney, and it was wet and sloppy throughout. We reached the top of the Diamond at 1:15 p.m.

Here are a few details on our equipment:

Pitons — About 35 were carried, mostly of chrome-moly hardened steel, in sizes varying from knife-blades to large angles 2-1/2 inches wide. All but a few were removed.

Bolts — We placed 4 Star Dryvin expansion bolts, 3/8 inch diameter by 1-1/2 inches long, as belay anchors. They are solidly driven and, in contrast to rawl-drive compression bolts, should be reliable for a number of years. Future parties should not need to place additional bolts.

Rope — Aside from the hand lines used in the North Chimney, 6 ropes were used on the climb. All were 7/16 inch diameter nylon. The rope used for leading was 150 feet long, the others either 150 or 120 feet. Two of them were left fixed over pitches 2, 3 and 4 to facilitate retreat or rescue, and were removed later. A 1,200 foot rope, loaned by Holubar, was available for rescue from the top.

Food — Salami, pepperoni, canned chicken, raisins, chocolate, and 4 quarts of water.

Bivouac Gear — Two down jackets (one Lionel Terray, one Sporthaus Schuster), sweaters, gloves, one Holubar waterproof parka and leg-bag, one poncho. These and the food were carried in a pack which we hauled up behind us."

The above report was also published in *Trail and Timberline* in the September, 1960 issue. With it was another article by Robert Kamps from which the following paragraph is quoted. It concerns the morning after the bivouac on the Diamond:

We realized that once we started in the morning, we had to make a crucial decision as our fixed line ran diagonally upward and outward to the left. We could leave a fixed rope from the upper bolt to the bivouac ledge. Otherwise, when we stepped into our prusik loops, and swung into space, retreat would be impossible. Should we cut off our retreat and find that the water-flowing, upper chimney was impassable, it would be up to our support party to help us. Trusting to our support we decided to do the latter.

Another article was written by David Rearick and published in *The American Alpine Journal*, 1961. The quotations from that article which follow will provide interesting highlights:

Back on the [bivouac] ledge it was getting cold, and we put on all of our clothes, some food, and tied in for the night. I sat in a cross-legged position all night, while Bob was able to recline partially. The night was clear and we watched the shadows from the moon creep stealthily along the slope of Lady Washington below us and across the shimmering blackness of Chasm Lake. We both managed to doze for a few hours . . . Several hardy newspaper reporters were on hand at the summit, and as we descended the regular route, we met others who had been defeated by the altitude at various levels.

In retrospect, the climb turned out to be somewhat harder than we had expected, because of the difficult rock in the central section. We never resorted to bolting for direct aid, our four expansion bolts being used only to anchor belays and prusik ropes. On the whole we were favored by the weather, which is undoubtedly the largest single factor in any climb on Longs Peak . . .

They spent 52 hours at the wall, of which 28-1/2 were used in actual climbing. There can be only one such "first." Johnson and Northcutt came close, but luck had continued against them. They and others had tried for years and made great efforts to get permission to attempt it. It was largely due to such continuous efforts that attention was directed to the Diamond, that resistance was broken down, and that it was at last opened to climbing. Then it was very disappointing to them and to their friends, that the final decision came at an inopportune time for them, and local climbers lost the honor of a "first."

Thus it was that Kamps and Rearick got first crack at the crack, and oh, what a crack that is! They were lucky enough to be ready when the opportunity came, and as it was said, they "aced" out the Colorado climbers. That should make it the Ace of Diamonds climb, it being also excellent and outstanding.

As an interesting aftermath, there promptly appeared secondary articles by the reporters pointing up the exhaustions and the aches which they themselves had suffered in order to watch and photograph the climb. They had comfortable beds but little time for sleep because they arose before dawn each day to "climb" from the base of the peak. Then after wearily retreating each night, they had to prepare and transmit their stories and pictures. Horseback riding added to their soreness and discomforts. They "climbed" much more than the climbers, took the worst beating, and were not doing it for sport.

Reporters also gave the National Park rangers credit for always being in "the right place at the right time," and with a portable radio to report progress or difficulties, and to secure more aid if needed. Chief Ranger Lyle McDowell, ranger Bob Frausen, and Longs Peak rangers John Clark and William Colony, were those upon whom much might have depended in the event of troubles. In 1962 when the Diamond was next to be attempted, David Rearick was, himself, a Longs Peak ranger. An article also praised the support party and the help that they gave without which "the climb could not have been made." (Quotations from *Rocky Mountain News*). The support party also brought down the gear, which was much appreciated by the climbers, who as "Kings of the Diamond" shared with the "Queens of the Rooftop Rodeo" the places of honor in the local rodeo parade the next day.

Rearick afterwards wrote the writer, "I have an old copy of your guidebook dating from 1946. It was a source of inspiration to me in the days when climbing the cable route represented the ultimate adventure. My father and I finally reached the summit of Longs Peak in 1950 after two unsuccessful attempts in 1944 and 1947." And so, my readers, if you are not successful the first time you try Longs Peak, or some other things, do not be discouraged. Your failures may be the stepping-stones upon which you develop the determination and the ability to succeed.

The 1960 climb took some of the edge off of the Diamond, and no one attempted to further polish it in 1961. In 1962, Johnson, still determined to win over the Diamond by his long-planned route, similar to that of Kamps and Rearick, made an attack with John Wharton, from England but teaching in Princeton, NJ. They started on Tuesday, August 7th, and spent the night on the two-foot-and-less ledge (*photo page 33*) just above the Ramp. The next morning, Wharton, who had reportedly had only ten days to become acclimated, was too ill to climb. Johnson advanced another 100 feet upward, hoping that by then Wharton might feel better, but he did not and they had to descend, and face another disappointment.

Morning moon over the summit.

Photo by — Lloyd O. Timblin Jr.

The Yellow Wall
(Second Diamond Climb)

Attention turned quickly to another attempt. This was planned by Layton Kor, Boulder bricklayer, who had done three other firsts on Longs and had been living and working between times for his rock-climbing trips. These had taken him all over the west to various climbs on Devils Tower, the Teton Mountains, Yosemite (including the face of Half Dome), the Bugaboos in Canada, Fishers Towers (see *The National Geographic Magazine* of November, 1962), Spider Rock, the Totem Pole, and Black Canyon, as well as new routes on the face of Chiefshead and the south side of Sharkstooth nearby. Give that man enough rope and he'll hang — in stirrups, and make first ascents most anywhere.

Two others were certified for this climb, Robert Culp of Boulder, and Jim McCarthy of Princeton, N.J. However, Culp became ill the day before, seemingly from a virus, and McCarthy was similarly too ill to climb on the appointed morning, Saturday, August 11th, although he had helped Kor to make a start of a few pitches the afternoon before. So it happened that Charles Roskosz, a mathematics student from Boulder, a member of the Diamond support party for the second time, became the other member of the team. His wife at home didn't even know he was climbing until she read it in the paper. Just think how much that shortened her worries!

This second climb of the Diamond started about 150 feet to the left, or southeast, of the first Diamond climb and was on a smoother, more yellowed section which they named the Yellow Wall. Here the rocks are very nearly vertical, rather than leaning outward as they do above the Ramp. There are fewer overhangs and the rock is more solid, but the crack system is not as continuous and more delicate traverses were therefore necessary.

Piton by piton, direct aid and tension, they pushed slowly upward, pitch after pitch, and then it happened. A piton on which Kor was standing gave way and instantly he started to drop. The next piton held, and through it and others, the rope in the expert hands of Roskosz stopped the fall. A "swami belt" of three or so wraps of nearly two-inch wide nylon webbing about his waist took the shock and eased the jerk and the cutting action which the rope might have caused.

"I gotcha, old man," said Roskosz as reported by the *Rocky Mountain News*. Later, Kor replied in answer to reporters' inquiries, "It all happened so fast, I didn't have time to get scared. I was a little shaky for the next five minutes though."

On one traverse especially, after using their knife-blade pitons and "RURPS" "Realized Ultimate Reality Pitons," developed and named by Yvon Chouinard, with short blades for tight, hairline cracks, they made use of ordinary pitons which could be driven only a little way in, and thus could not bear the leverage caused by support from the eye-holes at a distance from the rocks. This made it advisable to use an older device of winding lighter alpine cord around the shanks of the pitons and right next to the rock and supporting the stirrups from these points. This sufficed. Shortly thereafter they could "relax."

What would it be like sitting out such a night, trying against great odds and cold realities to rest and doze? What kind of "wall-eyed," nightmarish impressions might one have as his mind fitfully slips back and forth from waking to sleeping under the overwhelming dominance of that great wall which would tilt all of a flatlander's ways on edge? What thoughts might go through one's activated mind in his wakeful stretches on such an aerie perch, always conscious of that great space beside, that awful depth below, that looming height above, and that edge so near? A partial answer may come to the ordinary person who can imagine banishing clinging fears of height and replacing them with the climber's sense of elation, which results from the mastery of difficulties. The climber has great respect for exposure, but has learned to live with it. The discomforts of cramped positions become only incidents which give way to greater feelings of accomplishment.

Times of sleeping may be interrupted by the realization that the rope is cutting tighter, that in relaxation one has slumped nearer the brink, and that it is time to change position in order to avoid stiff muscles. Thus there will be some squirming, some flexing and rubbing of arms and legs, some shivering from the near freezing cold, and some thoughts of thirst to be controlled, for one does not lug up as much water as it would be nice to have.

In wakeful moments, the climber may be planning what to do for this or that problem which may lie above; contemplating the grandeur of the rugged surroundings, the brightness of the stars, the weather, the memories of other bivouacs, perhaps on desert towers on mild nights and without publicity, the many lights on the plains, and the comforts of home to be relished again after the climb.

The sun strikes the Diamond as soon as it rises and one can peer down through its ruddy rays into dark shadowed areas. Its warmth is soon felt by the impatient climbers, eager to be active and climbing again.

"Hey, let's eat and get going and get ahead of the afternoon storm." The warm-up proceeds with squirming, tensing of muscles, careful swinging of arms and stomping. Always watching balance, always close to the wall. Breakfasting on concentrated food, rationing out some water, stowing away the stuff, arranging packs and camping gear, methodically, carefully. Each carried about 30 pounds or less at the start, including three 150 foot ropes between them.

Eager to be actively meeting the challenge and achieving again, they started the climb. Kor led a pitch. Let us now listen to some of the sound effects to better help us to get the feel of the climb. At intervals in the background from Chasm View will come the extraneous, magnified voice of the radio contact with Park headquarters.

"On belay," shouted Kor, now anchored to the rock beside him and giving the signal that he was braced against any possible fall and ready to take up the rope as Roskosz climbed. "Climb," he shouted after a tug on the rope allowed him to feel the security of his position. "Climbing," replied Roskosz as he started upward, avoiding the use of the rope as a climbing aid. There were scraping noises from movements against the rock, grunting, puffing, knocking of pitons back and forth as he worked to get them out, metallic releasing noises as they came, and tinkling, jangling noises as he snapped them and carabiners to the piton belt around his waist.

Up to Kor and a careful, cautious changing of positions. The jangling hardware is handed over to Kor, who is now eager for exercise to get his blood circulating more actively again. The signals continue: "On belay." "Off belay." "Climb." "Climbing." "Slack" (more rope needed). "Up rope" (pull up slack). "Tension" (keep rope tight). Throughout could be heard the rising pitch of the "pings" of the pitons as they were driven in, or the "tongs" of the larger, lower pitched **bong bongs** for wider cracks (*photo page 33*).

So they progressed, at times the belayer standing in stirrups hung by carabiners to pitons on the side of the wall, a tiresome position if long maintained as is usually necessary, and over awesome exposure of hundreds of vertical feet. By 11 o'clock the sun has left the Diamond and it becomes cold at that altitude in the shade.

A short thunderstorm burst upon the mountain and sent rivulets splashing down over them. They tied on to their pitons, thus freeing their hands from the numbing cold of having to hang on. In a few minutes it immobilized them and then left the rocks wet and more slippery. They topped out just before 1 o'clock after 28-1/2 hours on the Yellow Wall, nineteen of them spent in climbing. To this figure must be added another five or so of pushing up the start on the previous day. They carried expansion bolts, but made the whole climb without making use of any.

After the climb, Roskosz was summoned to appear before the local U.S. Commissioner. He was charged with climbing the Diamond without having received permission. This, as will be remembered, was because two other certified climbers got sick, one at the last moment. Roskosz substituted and made the climb. He pleaded guilty and was assessed a small fine.

In June of 1963 and until July 3, Layton Kor and Floyd "Tex" Bossier of the Colorado Guide Service of Boulder made first ascents on the following new routes: Gray Pillar, Red Wall, Zig Zags, Crack of Delight, and Diagonal Directissima.

Then on July 6, 1963, with Royal Robbins, Kor reclimbed the Ace of Diamonds, or Diamond 1, in 16 hours. Just one week later, the same two pioneered a new route, the Jack of Diamonds, a few feet to the right. This was also accomplished in one long day of about 16 hours.

"Both climbs were properly approved and completed without incident or undue publicity," reported Allyn F. Hanks, superintendent.

In mid-August of 1964, the fifth successful climb of the Diamond was made. This was accomplished by Bob Boucher of Denver and Pat Ament, 17, of Boulder. They took two days and named the climb "The Grand Traverse." Some other attempts on the Diamond were turned back by bad weather.

Are these Diamond routes the hardest in the country? Of course not, although they are among the hardest to date. Harder climbs will yet be made. The Diamond, besides being quite uniformly sheer, lies entirely above 13,100 feet and is thus a colder adversary and more taxing upon one's physical stamina than most in our 48 contiguous states. Colorado's peaks in summertime tend to make their own local and more unpredictable thunderstorms with their special problems. However, the snow and ice and their particular hazards that are commonly found on high mountains are of little importance here in August, except for the crossing of Lambs Slide by novices.

Layton Kor, one of the most capable mountaineers to climb on Longs Peak, has said that "Mountains are God's gift to man. Experience is the most essential element in mountain climbing. Don't try to short-cut on it nor on safety. Live your climbing. Live a lot of it. Climb and climb, but get the experience gradually and thoroughly as you do. Of course a climber must dare to take some risks. And if continued long enough, some risks will result in failure. When one looks at a wall or starts to explore a route, he can tell if he can do it. The wall itself will do a great deal of discouraging and will sort out those who are not ready for it. A fellow will decide that it is not for him, because it may take a terrific lot of nerve and self-confidence. One can fail psychologically as well as physically."

It would seem that after many successful climbs of the Diamond and many other difficult routes on Longs Peak, without any recent fatalities to technical rock-climbers, the Park Service has weathered a critical stage. They may henceforth be less blamable, should there be a tragic fall. But how they might have suffered if the first attempt at the Diamond had resulted in tragedy! Public opinion would have been prone to say, "They had the power to prevent it. They should not have permitted them to risk their lives."

Now, however, these climbers have demonstrated that they really do know a great deal about what they are doing. As with astronauts, there are risks, but successes have shown that what was long impossible can now be accomplished by means of technical know-how.

The public is becoming more interested and informed concerning the accomplishments of this great sport of mountain climbing. Let us hope that the successes of the few experts do not overstimulate large numbers of unprepared emulators to attempt crags beyond their abilities, with resulting falls to the dismay and horror of horizontally-bound contemporaries, who seem to prefer to be crushed and snuffed out by the thousands in automobiles.

Henceforth, whenever one looks at that great Diamond, so well displayed in its natural setting, let it be a reminder of the great difficulties which can be overcome and of the heights to which human beings can ascend. Let us remember what Powell so aptly stated on the occasion of his first ascent of Longs Peak, that we have many "impossible routes" which need to be pioneered in other fields as well (see page 4).

Let those who gaze at the Diamond recognize the power of free individuals and of team work, and then say of whatever in other fields they have hesitated to try, but wanted very much to do, "It can be done."

Quotations, Mostly Gleaned from the Registers

- "Of all glad words mid start and stop, The gladdest of these — we've reached the top."
- From "Jacksonville, Florida — where there are no mountains ... God's Country."
- "A good gang — A stiff climb — A wonderful view — But a - - - - long way back"
- "8-17-33 We were caught in several blizzards coming up the cable route."
- "Ft. Worth, Texas. Just a mole hill — What good is it?"
- "7-26-35 Boy, is it cold and snowing"
- "Never again, at least not for two or three days."
- "Gambled in Reno all nite Tues. Drove all nite Wed. from Salt Lake. Here this 3:00 AM. Friday. Hope there's no more radical time up. About all in."
- "Elevator out of order. Boy are my dogs tired."
- "Will power is wonderful."
- "Longs Peak must be called that because it is a long way off."
- "Worth every moan and groan."
- "1 couldn't eat, but I'm living high."
- "I wore my heavy shoes so I wouldn't be blown away."
- "Take nothing but pictures. Leave nothing but tracks."
- "Halfway to heaven, but only a misstep from hell."
- "I thought I'd have to duck when I saw a satellite coming, but the Peak has learned to squat and let them pass."
- "I climbed Longs again to be sure I hadn't left anything. I hadn't."
- "The wilderness of the mountains is better than the bewilderness of the towns."
- "The mountains are the beginning and the end of all natural scenery." — John Ruskin
- Said of the first Diamond climb: ". . . a fairly difficult way to get up to where there isn't anything." — *The Denver Post.*
- "The Diamond, a giant slab that is a stern taskmaster and a stone-cold adversary." Corral Dust, *Estes Park Trail.*
- "A mountain is a friendly thing; it heals the hurts that cities bring." — Anon.
- "My last mountain. I'm done."

"RURPS"
Tinkle, tinkle little rurps.
A wonder that you hold my stirrups,
Up above the world so high,
On the Diamond near the sky!

- "One thing mountains never have is fear, Man brings that with him." — Bud Palmer
- "The mountains shall bring peace to the people." — Psalms 72:3.
- "There are old climbers and there are bold climbers, but there are no old, bold climbers." — Paul Petzoldt.
- "A mountain demands the utmost in individual responsibility, both for oneself and for his partner." — Bud Palmer.

Various Routes

The illustrations marked with lines of ascent, and the table which follows, giving numerous routes and variations, are an indication of the wealth of climbing possibilities on Longs Peak. These are presented, however, with some misgivings, for it is realized that the information given is entirely inadequate. In fact, no description, however thorough, would be enough to ensure safe climbs by enthusiasts who attempt routes beyond their ability. It cannot be too strongly emphasized that it is under the actual leadership of an experienced guide or climber that these routes can best be explored. To compensate for those who may become overly ambitious, this booklet is full of words of caution. So also is likely to be the advice of rangers and local residents, who have in mind some of the foolish things that have been done, and the resulting tragedies.

Fortunately, there are routes of many degrees of difficulty, and climbers are urged to practice on the easier routes and work up gradually to the more difficult. This will apply also to expert climbers in regard to their first climbs of each season while they get into condition, or their first climbs on Longs Peak, while they get acquainted with the type of rock and conditions presented.

With the above in mind, and starting with a previous rating by Field, an attempt has been made to arrange the various routes in order of difficulty, although it must be realized that the results are necessarily approximate. Only with the help of the combined opinions of various climbers has this task been undertaken. Information helpful in preparing the table has been received from Zumwalt, Wickens, Whitney, Walton, Smith, Ormes, Moomaw, Long, Kiener, Hornsby, Hornbein, Hart, Greeley, Gorrell, Frauson, Field, Eubank, Crowell, Craig, Carter, Buchtel, Brinker, Blaurock, Lamb, Gorman, Kor, Northcutt, Johnson, Clark, Schobinger, Roskosz, and Van Diver, Weeding, Rearick, Kamps, Becker, Bossier, Jon Malander, Griffiths, Dalke, Ament, Kuncl, J. Brown, Hurley, Dick Smith, Fricke, Briggs, Wadman, and the writings of others.

This edition now lists the American Decimal System (ADS) number with each route (when known) to give the reader a further indication of the difficulties and conditions involved on the various climbing routes. The first number can range from Roman numeral I to VI and indicates the overall magnitude or challenge of the route, especially in regard to the amount of time used in any technical climbing portion of the route. Thus a "Grade I" climb may indicate a rather long non-technical climb or a short and usually rather easy technical climb. A Grade VI climb will present the most difficult climbing problems known to present-day climbers, with a climbing duration of over two days. Grade V climbs are presently the most difficult ones on Longs Peak, with most of them on the Diamond area of the East Face.

The next number can range from 1 to 5.14, and indicates how hard the most difficult lead or pitch of a "free" climbing route will be. Thus a Class 1 route will indicate trail hiking, or a 2 route bushwhacking off a trail, hands used for balance, and a 3 route is rock scrambling, where some hand holds may be used to aid in climbing. 1 through 3 routes are considered non-technical climbing under favorable climbing conditions. A class 4 route is usually considered technical and all but the most capable and experienced climbers will want a rope and possibly some pitons just in case. All 54 of Colorado's 14,000 foot peaks are Class 4 or easier, assuming easiest climbing routes are taken. All class 5.0 through 5.14 are technical climbs, without use of artificial climbing aid. A climb of 5.10 would have at least one pitch of extremely difficult "free" climbing.

The third designation, when used, in the ADS number system indicates the presence, if any, of pitches requiring the use of direct or artificial climbing aid (as opposed to "free" climbing routes). These numbers run from A1 to A5, with A1 designating desirably placed anchor points (nuts or pitons) to A5 designating anchor points of insecure and questionable value. Briefly defined, a "free" technical climb uses anchor points only to hold the climber in case he should fall, and an artificial or direct aid technical climb uses anchor points as a direct aid in ascending the route as well as for safety reasons in case of a fall.

An example of an ADS number would be V 5.8 A4 route, which would involve a highly challenging climb, perhaps lasting two days with very sophisticated climbing techniques used, with at least one "free" climbing pitch of 5.8 (very difficult) and at least one place where one or more A4 anchor positions (somewhat insecure) are likely to be needed for aid.

It is requested that any experienced climbers who do any of the unusual routes write the publisher and give a recommended rating according to the American Decimal System. The opinions of several will help to give more valid ratings. Information on several of the older routes is inadequate and out-dated.

The Most Difficult Diamond Pitches
compiled by Roger Briggs, Boulder, Colorado
Pitch • Rating • History (*indicates the first lead with no falls)

1. The Joker #2 •12c •Briggs (93), Levin (93), Chace (94), *Adams (94)

2. Eroica #4 •12b •Briggs-Doub (87), Chace (88), Briggs (89), Lester-Doub (93)

3. The Joker #4 •12a/b• Levin (93), *Adams (94)

4. D1 #6 •12a/b •*Briggs (80, 88), Chace (83), Donahue (94), others (?)

5. The Joker #5 •12a •Briggs (93), *Adams (94)

6. Ariana #1 •12a •*Briggs (83), Suzuki (87), others

7. Eroica #3 •11d (R) •*Briggs (86, 87, 88), Gilbert (89)

8. The Joker #6 • 11d (W) •*Briggs (94)

9. The Joker #3 • 11d •*Briggs (93)

10. Hidden Diamond • 11d •*Webster (85), Briggs (94), Slater (94)

11. King of Swords #5 • 11d •*Gilbert (88), Briggs (89), Hersey (90)

12. Diagonal Direct #5 • 11c/d(R) •*Fowler (80)

13. Diagonal Direct #6 • 11c/d(R) •*Briggs (87), Lester (94)

14. King of Swords #3 • 11c/d(R) •*Briggs (85)

15. Eroica #2 • 11c/d •*Briggs (86)

16. King of Swords #6 • 11c/d •*Briggs (85)

17. Eroica #5 • 11c/d •*Doub (87)

18. King of Swords #4 • 11c •*Stone (85)

19. D7 #4 • 11c • *Bachar (77)

20. Ariana #2 • 11c •*Brlggs (76)

21. Soma #1 • 11b/c(R) •*Briggs (94)

22. Obelisk #1 and #2 • 11b/c •*Reveley (78)

23. Eroica #1 • 11b •*Briggs (82)

24. Diagonal #2 • 11b •*Adams (76)

25. Yellow Wall #4 • 11b •*Stone (78)

26. Black Dagger #4 • 11a •*Ferguson (80)

27. Pervertical #4 •11a •*Sorensen (75)

EDITOR'S NOTE:
There are now in excess of 125 climbing routes on Longs Peak;
see Wadman in the Bibliography for recent data.

Tables of Routes and Variations on Longs Peak

The best established routes are listed below and on the following three pages (over a hundred are listed and/or pictured including Mount Meeker), and are arranged in each group in approximate order of difficulty, especially of the hardest pitches, and under favorable conditions. The first route is for the unguided and inexperienced, and is considered non-technical in most summer climbing seasons. On rare occasions, conditions remain cold enough through the summer that no route, even the Keyhole, is considered non-technical.

Continual revision is necessary. Not only are more and more difficult climbs being accomplished, but it is becoming more difficult to keep track of them and present them in simple form. Climbs which a few years ago were considered unusual now tend to be regarded as commonplace among the more experienced climbers. It is not that the routes are changing, but that the ability of the climbers has been improving rapidly. The opinions of the best climbers a few years back may be quite out of date.

Flank designations are
W=West, N=North, S=South, E=East Face, SP=Ships Prow, M=North Face of Mt. Meeker.

Class	Route	Flank	First Ascent By	Year	Comments
I 2	Keyhole - Homestretch	W&S	Brown, solo	1870	Safest, longer
	For all following routes, consult with a ranger in person				
I 3	Glacier Gorge - Trough	W	*unknown*		Tiring talus
I 3	Keps Couloir to Notch	S	Keplinger, *solo*	1868	Rough talus
I 3	Pagoda to Narrows	S	Brown, *solo*	1870	Join Narrows at west end
I 3	Wild Basin – Homestretch	S	Indians, Powell party	1868	Long, tiresome talus
I 3	Around Palisade (from Meeker)	S	*unknown*		Talus, lost altitude
I 3	Forty-Second St.	E	Toll?		Chasm to Lady Washington Ridge
I 3	South end of Broadway	E	Lamb, solo	1871	Don't start loose rocks onto those below
I 3	Glacier Ridge	E	*unknown*	1924	Rough rocks
I 3	Apron to Loft (or Saggle)	E	Toll?, Zimmerman?		Go left on ledges below Apron
I 4	Through Keyboard of the Winds	W	Brown, *solo*	1870	Variable, little used
I 4	Dunnings Ledges	E	Kiener	1926	South of Chasm Lake
I 4	North End of Broadway	E	Bruns, solo	1925	Loose rocks, Loose rocks,
I 4	Gorrell's Traverse	S	Zimmerman, solo	1919	70 yds SW from Notch
I 4	Lambs Slide	E	Lamb descent, solo / Alexander, solo	1871 / 1922	Use only when good snow covers ice
I 4	False Keyhole Ledge	N	*unknown*		Short variation
I 4	West Couloir	W	Pre Mills	Pre-1896	Not easy to find loose stones
I 4	Right route, Fifth Avenue	E	Toll?		Chasm to Lady Washington ridge

Class	Route	Flank	First Ascent By	Year	Comments
1 4	Kieners	E	Kiener	1924	Easiest, most popular East face route to summit
1 4	Notch Chimneys	E	Alexander and Moomaw	1922	First chimney right of notch couloir
1 4	Right Dovetail	N	Bruns & Ervin Wickens, solo	1925 1930	Hard to approach in late season
1 4	Fisherman's Fantasy	E	Gorrell & Hornsby	1947	Ledges, Chasm to B. F.
1 4	VanDiver's West Wall	W	VanDiver & Working	1958	Is north of other West Wall
1 4	Zumie's Chimney	N	Zumwalt & Long	1932	Wet. Some insecure holds
1 4	Little Notch	E	Blaurock	1922	Variation of Kieners
1 4	Thumb Route	E	Grant & Jones	1948	Ice in lower part
1 4	West Chimney off Narrows	S	Long & Zumwalt	1932	Short. Good rock. Don't slip
1 4	East Chimney off Narrows	S	Greeley, solo	1932	Big flakes. Lie-backs, jamming
1 5+	Mary's Ledges	N	Wickens & Gilman	1930	Slick lichens when wet
1 5+	Webbs Walk-up	N	Koch & Webb	1963	Use 150-foot rope 40 feet right of Ev's Chimney
1 5+	Ev's Chimney	N	Long & Wichens	1931	Wet. Scarce hand holds, one overhang.
1 5+	Van Diver's Fantasy	E	Van Diver, solo	1948?	Higher, left hand ending
1 5+	Moss Chimneys	N			
II 5+	Notch Couloir	E	Lamb ? Solo descent Alexander, solo	1871 1922	Loose rocks
II 5+	Left or direct Dovetail	N	Gorrell, Watson & Alene Wharton	1935	Avoid impasse to right of final pitch
II 5+	West Wall	W	Eubank and Van Diver	1950	Cold in a.m. Good belays
I 5.4	North Chimney	E	Bruns, solo	1925	Loose rock
I 5.4	Glendennings Arete	E	Glendenning, Crowell & Fay	1953	Solid slabs. Good belays
I 5.4	Southwest Ridge	SW	(Mills?) Alexander	1924	Good belays
I 5.5	Stepladder	E	Gorrell & Watson	1935	Keplingermay have tried
I 5.5	Slabs	E	*Unknown*	1930s	Chimneys and Dihedrals
II 5.5	Keyhole Ridge	NW	Mills? Alexander & Smith	? 1924	Variable routes, generally top & left.
II 5.5	Alexander's chimney	E	Zimmerman, solo Alexander	1919 1922	Take lowest traverse Moomaw
I 5?	Broadway cut-off	E	Gorrell & Field	1936	Vertical pitch
I 5?	Left Detour from Alexander's Chimney	E	Wickens & Sharp	1930	Repeated with var. by Glendenning & Frauson
N/A	Bruns West Face	W	Bruns, solo	1924?	Indefinite location
I 5.5	Bongalong	E	J. Brown and Smythe	1966	Just left of Alexander's Chimney
N/A	Zumies Couloir	E	*Unknown*		info needed
N/A	Lambs Right Fork	E	*Unknown*		info needed
II 5.5	Fields Chimney	E	Field & Gorrell	1936	Wet & mossy overhangs

Class	Route	Flank	First Ascent By	Year	Comments
II ?	Right Field	E	*Unknown*		Loose rock, unpleasant
I 5.6	Kuncl Direct	E	Deeming & Kuncl	1959	Cuts off Alex Trav.
II 5.6	Eighth route	E	Field, Gorrell & Hauk	1940	Loose rock, hard at top
I 5.6	Rollyco Stair	E	Ament & Dalke	1964	Low. Left of 5th Avenue
II 5.7	Chasm cut-off, Ledge Rt.	E	Eubank, Van Diver, & Hornbein	1950	Exposed rotten place on traverse
II 5.6 A1	Schobinger Cracks	E	Schobinger and Amato	1958	Bypasses Window directly to Eubanks Chimney
I 5?	Fourth of July	W	King and Gusthurst	1963	Obvious Open-Book crack
N/A	East Arete	N	Becker, Gorman and Gustafson	1955	Flank M is on Mt. Meeker
I 5.7	Fricke Trash Patrol	E			Behind chock stone, ice.
II 5.7	Swayback	N	Ament & Pfahler	1964	"Enjoyable slab climbing"
II 5.7	Stettner's Ledges	E	J & P Stettner's	1927	Exposed. Use short leads
II 5.6	Joe's Solo	E	J. Stettner, solo	1935	Exposed
N/A	Chasm cut-off, Chimney Rt.	E	Gregg & Carey	1950	Hard pitches
I 5.?	Right Detour from Alexander's Chimney	E	Eubank and Van Diver	1948	Small holds, exposed
II 5.7 A1	Nexus Corner	SP	Burbank and Shepherd	1964	Left of Stromboli
II 5.?	Weedings Detour	E	Weedings, Raves and Auten	1952	Drier than Fields Chimney
II 5.6	Great Chimney	S	Camp Hole Climbers	1957	Classic chimney work
III ?	Cobra	N	Layton Kor		Four hours
II 5.7	Stromboli	SP	Lamb, Jackson, & Gorman	1954	40 ft. from east profile
N/A	South Corner from Window	E	Green, Gustafson, Clark & Ridsdale	1953	Escapes farther to left when chimney is bad
II 5.7	Window Route (Eubanks Chim. end)	E	Eubank and Van Diver	1950	Delicate slab work. Unprotected chock stone at top
III 5.7	Tiptoe	E	Oulette and Woodford	1956	Exposed. One delicate pitch
II 5.7	Crack of Delight	E	Bossier & Kor	1963	3 hours free climbing
II 5.7	Window Direct	E	Johnson & Huston	1958	N. Bdwy dir. to window
III 5.7 A1	Malanders' Passage	E	Jim and Jon Malander	1963	Repeated w/out aid
II 5.8	Craigs Crack	E	Craig, R. Whitney, H. Whitney	1952	Exposed, many pitons
II 5.8	Hornbein Crack (Chasm view)	E	Hornbein and Huston	1953	40 ft. unprotected lieback
I 5.8	Hornsbys Direct Finish	E	Hornsby and Walton	1949	From Stettners Ledges
III 5.8	Big Toe	E	Carter & Auld	1959	Tiptoe Variation
III 5.8A1	Flying Buttress	N	Reppy, Carey & Arsegi	1963	Graceful arete
III ?	Shining Slab	S	Burbank and Shepherd	1963	Maybe ended in Fields Chimney

Class	Route	Flank	First Ascent By	Year	Comments
III 5.9	Zumie's Buttress	E	Schrobinger & Amato	1959	Involved bivouac
III 5.9	Zumies Thumb (now 3 variations)	E	Hornbein, Brinker, Waldrup	1951	Exposed friction pitches. Not a summit route
II 5.9	Upper Indirectissima	E	L. Dalke & Jennings	1967	Harder free climbing
II 5.7 A1	Kors Door	E	Kor and Hough	1958	Exposed, some tension
II 5.7 A2	Indirectissima	E	Fricke & Glidden	1967	
III 5.9 A1	Eclipse	E	Ament & Boucher	1963	"Classic dihedrals & slabs"
II 5.9 A1	Portal	S	Boucher and Shephard	1963	Just right of Stromboli
II 5.7 A2	Zig Zags	E	Bossier and Kor	1963	Arching, inside corners
II 5.8 A2	Chosen View	E	Carter and Smith	1953	Six feet right of crack. Tension Finish
III 5.7 A3	Concave	N	Kor & Larry Dalke	1968	Rock route farthest left
III 5.7 A3	Overhang Dihedral	E	Ament & Kor	1964	
IV 5.6 A3	Hypotenuse	E	Hurley & Hough	1968	At left edge of Diamond
II 5.9 A3	Peacock Wall	N	Ament & Schaefer	1965	Above Peacock Pool
N/A	Nose of Ships Prow	SP	Kamps & Laughlin	1960	Conditioner for Diamond 1
IV 5.7 A2	Red Wall	E	Bossier & Kor	1964	Strenuous, 6 1/2 hours
III 5.8 A2	Directissima	E	Kor and Lagrange	1960	Vertical crack
II 5.9 A4	Step One	SP	Ament & Pfahler	1964	"Short but sweet and steep"
III 5.7 A3	Nassawand	E	Covington, Hickman	1969	Rappel at end
III 5.7 A4	Gang Plank	S	Ament & Robbins	1963	Sheer wall
IV 5.7 A4	Striped Wall	E	Goss & Kor	1965	Dangerous from falling rocks
IV 5.7 A4	Invisible Wall	E	Dalke & Kor	1965	Difficult aid
V 5.6 A2	Diamond 7 (D-7)	E	L. Dalke, Goss, Hurley	1966	Most climbed Diamond route
V 5.6 A3	Curving Vine	E	Covington & Robinson	1966	Two pendulum pitches & bivouacs
V 5.7 A3	D Minor 7	E	Bradley & Petrillo	1967	Left-hand variation of D-7
V	Dunn	E	Dunn & Westbay	1971	"No harder than D-7"
V 5.7 A3	Enos Mills Wall	E	Kor & Goss	1967	Midway bivouac
V 5.7 A3	Black Dagger	E	R. Dalke & Goss	1967	Through small black gash in wall
V 5.8 A3	Forrest's Finish	E	Forrest	1970	First solo on Diamond
V	Waterhole No. 3	E	Walker	1971	Much falling water
V 5.7 A4	Gray Pillar	E	Bossier & Kor	1963	Hard granite
V 5.7 A4	Diamond 1	E	Kamps & Rearick	1960	See story on p. 52
V 5.7 A4	Diagonal Direct	E	Bossier & Kor	1963	14 hrs. in bad weather
V 5.9 A3	Diagonal	E	Northcutt, Kor (& Lamb)	1959	Includes Long Dihedral
V 5.8 A4	The Grand Traverse	E	Ament & Boucher	1964	Longest route on Diamond
V 5.8 A4	Yellow Wall	E	Kor & Roskosz	1962	See story on p. 55
V 5.9 A4	Jack of Diamonds	E	Kor & Robbins	1963	"I'll take the Queen"

Interesting Events and Dates Concerning Longs Peak

See also tables of routes and fatalities

1820, Jun. 30: First recorded sight of Longs Peak by exploring party headed by Major Stephen H. Long and approaching from the Great Plains.

1868, September: installation was completed of a 280-foot telescope with a reflector 16 feet in diameter, on the summit of Longs Peak. This was accomplished to watch the progress of the first projectile trip to the moon after it was fired from Florida. Author of this fiction was Jules Verne, who described it in his story, *From the Earth to the Moon.*

1867, September: Kit Carson, Col. Dick Rutledge, Capt. Wm. F. Drennan, Tob Tobin and 10 friendly Indians came to see how the beaver trapping was in the Estes Park region. An old cabin site in the Tahosa Valley was credited to them.

1868, August 23: First authenticated climb to summit. Party led by Major J. W. Powell. Other members were: W.N. Byers, W.H. Powell, L.W. Keplinger, Samuel Gorman, Ned E. Farrelo, and John C. Sumner. See January 1968 *Trail and Timberline*. Also December, 1951.

1870, August 2: Donald Brown made first solo climb, taking four days from Estes Park.

1871, August: The Rev. Elkanah J. Lamb made the first descent of the East Face.

1873: Addie Alexander of St. Louis was the first woman on the Peak (according to W. Gorrell)

1873, September 13: Miss Anna E. Dickinson was for long supposed to be the first woman to climb the Peak. She accompanied the Hayden Survey party and others. Mt. Meeker and Mt. Lady Washington were named on this trip. She had climbed Mt. Washington, N.H., 27 times.

1873, October: Much publicized climb of Isabella Bird, "Rocky Mountain Jim" (Nugent), Platt Rogers and S.S. Downer. Miss Bird was the author of *A Lady's Life in the Rocky Mountains.*

1876: E. J. Lamb and son Carlisle cleared a roadway past Lily Lake into Tahosa Valley, east of Longs Peak, and erected some crude buildings for summer use at the site of Longs Peak Inn.

1878: E. J. Lamb established permanent home and accommodations for climbers, and became the first regular guide. Way cleared to get horses above timberline.

1880, August: Geoge B. McFadden and six out of 12 members of Longmont Cornet Band got to the top and played through a specially printed program of band music.

1882: The Lambs completed the first trail. It stayed north of Alpine Brook.

1885: Enos A. Mills first climbed.

1887: Frank L. Hornbaker started guiding parties from Boulder, Colorado, to the top of Longs Peak. They took a train to Ward, a stage to Meeker, and then horses to Boulderfield.

1887, August: Frederick H. Chapin in *Mountaineering in Colorado* reports that about 100 people have climbed Longs Peak annually for several years past.

1896, August: First moonlight climb by H. C. Rogers.

1900: Large, separate forest fires on both north and east flanks.

1900, Sept. 3: Mrs. E. J. Lamb climbed the day before her 70th birthday, guided by E. J. Lamb and accompanied by Enos A. Mills, Editor McGuire of *Outdoor Life* and four others, including Mrs. F. S. (Harriet A.) Huntington, whose birthday coincided with Mrs. Lamb's and who reports: "Aunt Jane was like a cricket, so bright and active and the first to the top that day," and on the descent, "I indulged in too much ice water and developed a raging headache. Aunt Jane doctored me, 70 years administering to a girl of 19, and I soon was better."

1901 and 1902: Party of students under Prof. L. G. Carpenter of the Colorado Agricultural College determined the exact altitude by leveling to the summit, 14,255 feet high.

1902: Enos Mills purchased Lamb's Long Peak House and renamed it Longs Peak Inn.

1903, February: First winter climb by Enos A. Mills.

1905: Townsite of Estes Park laid out.

1905, Sept. 23: Eugenia Mine lode was discovered. It was worked for a few years thereafter, and the title held through 1919, according to Harold Dunning. Its mineral value is doubtful.

1906: Enos Mills reported guiding 32 ascents during August, six of them by moonlight.

1907: Shep Husted reported 50 ascents of Longs Peak, 27 of them in August

1908: Timberline Cabin established by Enos Mills. Abandoned after 1924.

1914: Hewes-Kirkwood Inn established by Charles E. Hewes, Steve B. Hewes, and their mother, Mrs. Kirkwood.

1915 Jan. 28: Rocky Mountain National Park created. Longs Peak included.

1915, July 18: Colorado Mountain Club register placed on the summit and since maintained for all to sign.

1919, Aug. 23: Werner Zimmerman, Bern, Switzerland (CAS.), wrote as follows in the register: "Alone. Traverse east west by abyss chimney 20 yards south." With only this as a clue, it was discovered that Mr. Zimmerman is well-known in Europe as a world traveler, writer and lecturer and has done considerable climbing in different areas. His book, *Weltvagant*, tells of his Longs Peak climb and he has marked photographs for me, showing his ascent to have been via Alexander's Chimney and the Eighth Route and thence via Gorrells Traverse.

1920 to 1925: Entire trail from Longs Peak Campground relocated and remade under the direction of rangers Dean Babcock and Jack Moomaw. Followed Mills Moraine.

1922, Sept. 7: The East Face ascended by Prof. J. W. Alexander of Princeton.

1922, Sept. 10: Mrs. Herman Buhl was the first woman to climb the East Face.

1924, July 24: Abner Sprague, at the age of 74, walked from Sprague's Lodge to the top and back in one day, on the 50th anniversary of his first ascent.

1925, Jan. 12: First ascent of the East Face in winter by Walter Kiener and Agnes Vaille. Tragic deaths of Agnes Vaille and of Herbert Sortland, member of a rescue party.

1925, July 17: Longs Peak Trail completed from the edge of Boulderfield to its center, and telephone line installed, both under the direction of Jack Moomaw.

1925, July 25: Guy Caldwell (guide), Cy Neville, and Jack Lively were the first to climb and descend the East Face in one day.

1925, Sept. 3: Cables completed on the North Face under the direction of ranger Jack Moomaw. Lower cable 160 feet. Upper cable 30 feet.

1926: Trail extended from Mills Moraine to Chasm Meadows.

1926, Sept 2: Oldest person, the Rev. William Butler of Longmont, walked to the summit and back from Hewes-Kirkwood Inn on his 85th birthday.

1927, June 14: First and only marriage on top of Longs Peak. Lucille Goodman and Burl Stevens were married in snowstorm by the Rev. Charles E. Hannan. Paul Nesbit, guide.

1927: Bouderflcld Shelter Cabin and stable completed by the National Park Service and operated by Robert Collier, Jr., 1927 through 1935. Demolished, June 1937. Keyhole Shelter Cabin constructed in memory of Agnes Vaille.

1927, July 19: Two Iowa boys were rescued after spending the night on a narrow ledge atop the East Face, which they had intended to descend.

1930: Completion of new road to Bear Lake and of trail from Bear Lake which joins the other at Granite Pass.

1930s: Sometime in the 30s, Baker Armstrong of Camp Audubon near Brainerd Lake led a party of 50 boys to the summit of Longs Peak and got them all back without mishap.

1930, Sept. 1: Betty Dunning of Loveland, youngest girl to climb. Age five years, eight months and 29 days.

1931, Aug. 13-14: Francis W. Chamberlin, Lincoln, Nebraska, was the first to climb to the summit with crutches and but one leg and without assistance.

1931, Aug. 30-31: First all-night ascent of East Face. Ev Long, Carleton Long, Melvin Wickens, and Mrs. Dorothy D. Collier. Clouds obscured moon. Had flashlight, but did not have to use it. Greater safety, because fewer falling rocks.

1931: 2132 signatures in the summit registers. Greatest number till 1954.

1931: Chasm Lake Shelter Cabin constructed.

1932, Jan. 1: Second of two New Years climbs by Dorothy Crouter, Lyons, CO., teacher.

1932: Clerin Zumwalt, Boulderfield guide, made 53 climbs in one year. It was common for such guides to make two or three trips a day, but see next item.

1932, Sept. 9: Clerin Zumwalt and Hull Cook, "From Boulderfield via Bear, Fern, Tonahutu, Grand Lake, Lake Verna, Wild Basin: 55 miles"

1933, Aug 25: Jack Ladd of Loveland, Colorado youngest boy to climb. Age less than five years eight months.

1935, Aug. 20: George Greeley climbed to summit by four different routes in one day. First he took a party up the cables and later in the day singled on three consecutive lines: "Via West Couloir, via S.W. Ridge, via West Chimney off Narrows."

1935, Aug. 21: First live non-commercial two-way radio broadcast at 56,000 kilocycles from the top of Longs Peak by Art and Bob Tschannen. They talked to ham operators W9HWR in Longmont and W9PWU in Arvada.

1936, Jan. 1: Ernie Field made his fifth consecutive New Year's Day climb, this time alone. "Summit in clouds; about five above zero. Very difficult climbing on North Face. Icy. Moderate west wind"

1938: Ernie Field assigned as first special Longs Peak seasonal ranger.

1939, Jan. 1: First solo climb of East Face in winter made by Edwin Watson of Denver. This was the climax and the last in a series of consecutive January climbs, the first of which was by Jack Moomaw, Jan. 26, 1928. Many of these climbs were on New Year's Day. Stuart Clark, Jess Fults and Glenn Niner climbed from two to four times each.

1944: War-time conditions reduced the number of climbers to 622, the lowest number since 1920.

1948: Full "complement" of horse manure appeared on top. Must have been Pegasus.

1949, June 9: Famous, rustic, main building at Longs Peak Inn burned to the ground.

1949, Aug. 13: Thirteen climbed the regular route of East Face on four separate ropes. Consisted of nine boys 12 to 15 years of age and two of their teachers from New York's Lincoln School of Progressive Education. Otto Van Allman and Bob Fagan, guides.

1952, Aug. 31: Youngest person on top. Robert Riley, III, age 20 months, son of Bob Riley, guide. Perhaps the only person to ride up!

1953: Otto Van Allman, who guided for ten years from 1949 through 1958, signed 35 climbs to the top, a record for guides based at the foot since the registers were placed but equaled by himself in 1954. Only one other guide not based at Boulderfield has signed more than 22 times in one year: Glenn L. Mills (no relation to Enos), 31 times in 1916. Of Otto's climbs, 28 were via the East Face, more than double the number of any other East Face climber in one year. Twelve starts were made on 13 consecutive days, but two were rained out.

1953, July 15: A severe electrical storm moved in low from the northeast, burned two girls at the foot of the cables, others just above the cables, stunned or knocked down nine boys at the top of the Homestretch, a hiker on Battle Mountain, climbers above Loch Vale, and knocked out communications at Twin Sisters lookout. It is notable that the bolt which killed J. E. Kitts on the summit in 1922, and numerous lightning strikes once witnessed by the writer, also resulted from storms which moved in and upward from the east rather than from the usual westerly direction. It thus appears that more information should be secured about such easterly storms, and Longs Peak climbers should be wary of them, but meanwhile also respectful of those from the west.

1953, Aug. 8: James Ramsey Ullman, author of several books about mountains, climbed.

1954, Aug. 28: A 25-year-old law student walked into Meeker Park Campground on Saturday morning after becoming lost on Longs Peak the previous Sunday. He had climbed ahead of his group on the North Face in a storm. He did not find the register on top, and told that while descending the Keyhole Route in the clouds, he failed to follow the markers, became confused and wandered about the slopes of other mountains all week. Meanwhile, searchers on the ground and in the air examined the Peak and its approaches rock by rock and ledge by ledge in the most intensive hunt ever conducted on the mountain.

1954, Aug. 29: Nine climbed Stettners Ledges in one day with five of them continuing by the Window Route. Of these latter, George Lamb and Clifford Smith completed the climb in seven hours from Chasm Lake Shelter.

1954: Longs Peak climbed by 2,189, the greatest number in any one year, until 1966.

1955, Aug. 11: Largest party on top, 61 Boy Scouts from Camp Tahosa.

1957: Two rangers assigned to the Longs Peak Ranger Station for the first time.

1958: Bear Lake Lodge operated for its last season.

1959, June 27: A 21-year-old Boulder, Colorado, climber suffered a mental and physical collapse when caught in a severe storm. Ranger personnel fortunately encountered him near the summit and got him down to Agnes Vaille Shelter where they cared for him all night so that he had regained much of his strength by morning.

1959, Aug. 27: Cleve McCarty of Denver climbed Longs Peak, thus completing in 53 days the ascent of all 54 of Colorado's peaks then believed to be 14,000 feet or over.

1960, Aug. 3: The Diamond, smoothest and most vertical part of the East Face, first climbed by Robert Kamps and David Rearick, via the Diamond 1 route (*see page 51*).

1961, July 20: Eight inches of snow fell on Longs Peak. The whole season was colder and wetter than usual and only 785 made the climb. Perhaps the first year since the 40s with no regular guide.

1961, Aug. 16: A young couple signed out for the East Face. "They climbed to the Loft, crossed the upper end of Hunter Creek, passed over the ridge into Lion Lakes, crossed the Continental Divide twice, and then came out at Mills Lake and were found August 18." It would be easier for everyone if lost people would just sit down, or else just go downhill.

1962: Rocky Mountain Guide Service and Mountaineering School, Inc., began its first year of operation.

1962, Aug. 22: Second climb of the Diamond via the Yellow Wall route by Layton Kor and Charles Roskosz (*see page 55*).

1962, Aug. 19: The Colorado Mountain Club attempted simultaneous climbs of all of Colorado's 14,000-foot peaks, in observance of their 50th anniversary. Electrical storms turned back parties from six of them. Twelve members ascended Longs Peak, among them Paul Nesbit.

1963: Four members of the American Mount Everest Expedition, 1963, consider that climbing Longs Peak, sometimes in winter, provided an important part of their mountaineering interests or training. Their names and other duties besides being climbers are: Allen Auten, communications, power generation, and sound recordings; Barry Bishop, National

Geographic Society photographer and solar radiation measurements; Dick Pownall, in charge of food planning, and Lt. Cmdr. Thomas Hornbein, M.D., oxygen equipment and masks, and physiological studies.

Of the above, Tom Hornbein and Barry Bishop were among the first five Americans to reach the summit of Mt. Everest. Tom Hornbein had made difficult first ascents on Longs Peak, and stated, "More than any single area, the greatest part of my (climbing) experience was gained there:" Tom was also a local ranger-naturalist for a time. Longs Peak was the first 14,000-foot peak that Barry Bishop climbed as a boy. On this and two more later ascents, he was guided by the author. Barry more recently wrote, "I think that those fine summers with people like yourself were instrumental in making mountaineering my first avocation." Al Auten furnished final support for the West Ridge climbers. Dick Pownall helped the South Col support team (*Everest: The West Ridge* by Tom Hornbein, Norman Dhyrenfurth, and others. The Sierra Club, 1965).

1963: Three rangers assigned to Longs Peak Ranger Station for the first time.

1964, Aug. 15: 171 climbed and signed the register, the largest number in any one day.

1964, Aug. 22: Three generations of the Michener family climbed together over the N.W. Ridge. They were Dr. R.B. Michener of Iowa City, his sons Bryan and Bob, and grandson Eric, 13. The total number of climbs for the family is 101. It was Dr. Michener's 35th.

1964: 190 climbed the East Face, a record number for a long time.

1965, July 31: Eight inches of snow fell on the upper slopes of Longs Peak. The following day the author led a Colorado Mountain Club party of 15 on his snowiest summer climb. Only a few more than 100 had climbed so far that season. Ropes, ice axes, and crampons were used. Having ascended by the cables, it seemed easier and safer to descend the same way and use the same steps cut into the old hard snow than to negotiate the long, snow-filled Trough and the slippery Homestretch.

1965, Aug. 31: Dudley Smith and his son, Dudley, Jr., climbed via the Keyhole on the 50th anniversary of the father's first climb. It was his 18th. "This is a much longer trip than it was years ago!"

1965: Larger than usual snow banks and adverse weather reduced the number of climbs to 761, the lowest number since World War II years.

1966, Aug. 20-22: Larry Dalke, Wayne Goss and George Hurley made the first 3-man climb of the Diamond. It was a new route which they named D7. It was the seventh route on the Diamond and the seventh attempt to climb that one.

1966, Aug. 28: Brian Marts of the Rocky Mountain Climbing School and Guide Service, with great effort and daring, retrieved the body of C. Blake Hiester, Jr., from 250 feet down the *bergschrund* (ice crevice) at the foot of the East Face.

1966: 590 registered for technical climbs, many via the East Face, and the greatest number of any year. See Verne Huser's "The Summer of the Diamond" in the January-February 1967 issue of *Summit*.

1966, Oct. 3: Ranger Walter Fricke and another climber encountered bad snow conditions as they rappelled down Stettners Ledges. They had to stay all night and nearly perished, but they got down mostly on "Fricke power," much to the relief of a group of rescuers who had arrived.

1966, Dec. 25: Robert Culp and Wayne Goss attempted the first winter climb of the Diamond, but retreated because of bad weather. Then they helped Ranger Jerry Phillips and Jack Gartner search for three climbers who had gone up to photograph them.

1966, 1967: Climbers ascending Longs Peak about doubled over previous years, according to National Park Service records. Perhaps the method of counting changed.

1967, March 4 - with waiting - 12th: First successful winter ascent of the Diamond and by a new route, now called Enos Mills Wall, by Wayne Goss and Layton Kor. See Kor's "On the Granite Wall," in the June 1967 issue of *Trail and Timberline*.

1967: Twenty-one parties attempted the Diamond. Eleven succeeded, some on their second try.

1968, Jan. 27: Richard Kezlan tumbled down Lambs Slide, receiving a gaping head wound, skull fractures, bled profusely, and would have died that winter night excepting for some good luck. Dr. Dee Crouch happened to be at Chasm Lake Shelter Cabin. By means of shortwave radio which the party carried, Dr. Sam Luce of Estes Park arrived in six hours with a transfusion, more blood came a short time later, and 24 hours after the accident, helped by 37 people who became involved in getting him down, Kezlan was undergoing surgery at Colorado General Hospital. See Dr. Dee B. Crouch's "Midwinter Rescue on Longs Peak," in the March 1969 *Trail and Timberline*.

1968, Aug. 23: The National Park Service planned a climb on the 100th anniversary of the first ascent of Longs Peak by Major J. W. Powell and party. The more enthusiastic climbers camped at Sand Beach Lake, in order to ascend as Powell's party did from the south. The evening was fair, but a storm blew in. The next morning there was strong wind and snow on the ground. Ranger Walter Fricke spent the night on top. By portable radio he reported wind up to 70 miles per hour and a temperature near 15 degrees. All rocks were covered with snow and ice. Chief Ranger James Randall led a party of 14 to the top from Sand Beach Lake. Among them were two rangers' wives, Ruth Ann Smith and Ginger Jones, 13-year-old Brenda Mekeel, Michael Kiley, grandson of Enos A. Mills, and Dale Deffenbaugh, who had instigated an anniversary climb. The author and some National Park Service officials turned back at 8 a.m. from Boulderfield, thus following some advice they often give, "Turn back when conditions are not right." Neither did anyone else make the climb on the regular routes that day. That evening a steak barbecue was held in Wild Basin for those who reached the top, several former guides, rangers, old timers, and Park Service officials.

1968, Aug. 24: One hundred years and a day after L.W. Keplinger led the Powell party up a route he had found, six of his direct descendants climbed Longs Peak. They had disappointedly turned back the day before. They credited Emerson Lynn (who must have been 70) and his family with getting them to the top.

1968: The Diamond has to date been climbed successfully by at least 24 different parties, 34 different individuals and by nine different routes. Climbing restrictions have been relaxed. Of the routes that have been climbed more than once, D1 (The Ace of Diamonds) seems to be most dangerous, and D7 the easiest, safest, and most popular. In the last four years, there have been at least 31 unsuccessful attempts.

1968: Longs Peak had its greatest number of climbers, 4,226. Of these, 379 were registered as technical, mostly via the East Face.

1969, July 17: Edwin H. Paget, professor emeritus of North Carolina State University, said he climbed Longs Peak and Pikes Peak in the same day. Prof. Paget was over 65 years of age and advocated the delaying of old age by means of vigorous exercise. He hiked up Pikes Peak over 400 times in 50 years, made the hike up in three hours and ten minutes, and four times in one day by riding down. These later records are recent.

1969, Aug 2: Kordel Kor had a roped fall from the first lead on the Grand Traverse route of the Diamond and sustained serious head injuries, plus a fractured femur and kneecap. He was lowered in a Stokes litter from Broadway to Mills Glacier, carried to Chasm Lake Shelter, and evacuated by helicopter to a Boulder hospital. The seriousness and nature of the injuries and the method of rescue required to evacuate him from Broadway down the lower half of the East Face probably makes this the most arduous and complicated rescue to this writing.

1969, Aug. 16: The first trial rescue using a descent from the edge of the North Face down to a "victim" on the Diamond was successfully completed. This event used the latest mountain rescue techniques and answered many unknowns involved in evacuating an accident off the Diamond. 3,200 feet of rope were used to lower the Stokes litter to Mills Glacier, making it the longest single continuous lowering of a litter in the United State. 500 lbs. of rope and rescue gear were carried up the cable route to stage the "rescue." (see entry for September 6, 1992 for a litter rescue from the Trough to the summit)

1970: New telephone installed at Chasm Lake Shelter Cabin.

1970, July 26: First solo climb of the Diamond by William Forrest. He started with the Yellow Wall route and completed the climb with a new route called "Forrest's Finish."

1970, August: Fred Rainguet, Hikemaster at Camp St. Malo, led a group of 109 to the summit and back without incident, in very poor weather. The group ascended and descended by the north face cables, with counselors stationed along the route to provide assistance; this may well be a record.

1970, Aug. 2: Mrs. Johanna Marte is the first woman to climb the Diamond, along with Dr. Egon Marte and Mike Covington.

1971, July 25: First live commercial radio broadcast from the top of Longs Peak by Daryle Klassen with KLOV radio in Loveland, Colorado.

1971, Aug. 14: A daring and spectacular rescue of Chris Chidsey, who had broken his leg in a fall from Notch Chimneys just above Broadway on the East Face. The victim was placed in a *tragsitz* mounted on the back of Park Ranger Walter Fricke and evacuated in a single, continuous lowering of 850 feet down the sheer vertical rock face below Broadway. The 8-man rescue team was awarded the Department of the Interior's unit award for excellence of service, and in addition, Mr. Fricke received the Department of Interior's Valor Award.

1972: First helicopter landing on the summit.

1973, July 20: Cables removed from the North Face.

1975, July: First free climb of the Diamond (Wayne Goss and Jim Logan) to Table Ledge.

1975, July: First all-female Diamond climb (Atwood, Higgins and Manson).

1978: Briggs and Candelaria free climb entire Diamond.

1977: Cleve McCarty of Boulder and his 12-year-old son Eric bicycled to the trailhead, climbed Kieners route on the East Face (roped only at Mills Glacier), went down the North Face and biked home, all in one day.

1978, July Diamond 'Casual Route' free soloed by Charlie Fowler, without a rope.

1983, May: John Harlin III skied from the summit down the North Face. He also skied Notch Couloir in 1984.

1984: Jim's Grove closed to camping due to over-crowding.

1985: Roger Briggs brought the upper limits of 5.12 rock climbing to Longs Peak's Diamond with the freeing of the original D-1 route with Jeff Achey, Ariana with Bill Briggs, and the freeing of King of Swords (formerly Its Welx) with Dan Stone.

1988: Michael Smithson, a paraplegic, climbed the Peak via the North Face in 3 days.

1988, May 18: Jeff Wax, Salt Lake City, struck in buttocks by lightning.

1988, August: Two blind climbers, Martha Villa and Shirley Smith, climbed the North face.

1988, September The severity of the Western fires, particularly at Yellowstone National Park, caused park officials to barricade public access to all Rocky Mountain Park backcountry, including Longs Peak. The majority of park firefighters were sent outside the park on assignments. Longs Peak normally sees an average of one lightning-caused wildfire per year, which is usually promptly extinguished.

1989, June: Marcus Massari, age 4 years and 364 days, set a new record as the youngest person to climb Longs Peak under his own power. He was accompanied by his father, Joe Massari.

1989, July 10: English climber Derek Hersey climbed up the Yellow Wall, down the Casual Route, and up Pervertical Sanctuary, three Diamond climbs in one day, free solo without a rope. (Kids, don't try this at home!)

1990, July 29: Timothy Fromalt stopped his girlfriend from falling on the Homestretch during a lightning storm, but then fell sixty feet to his own death. Ranger John Gillett responded solo up and over the North Face during the severe lightning storm which pinned down the rest of the rescue team at the Keyhole. Gillett then performed CPR, assisted the physician-advisor with determining death via cellular phone, gave away his rain clothes to volunteer assistants, and assisted the injured girlfriend to the trailhead. He was awarded a commendation for his brave and selfless actions.

1990, September 5: Jim Mauch and Cathy Casey were stranded in the first winter storm of the season on Kiener's Route, A United States Army C-47 Chinook helicopter from Fort Carson, Colorado, was used to transport Mauch and Casey and their four ranger rescuers from the summit of Longs Peak. This was the largest aircraft ever to land on the Longs Peak summit (it is big enough to transport either 50 soldiers or a tank).

1990, November: Clay Wadman and Gordie Kito accomplish the first one day (22-1/2 hours) climb of the Diamond (D7) in winter conditions (but technically in autumn).

1991, April 20: Joe Massari fell 1500' from Upper Kiener's Route to Mills Glacier, and his body was buried by heavy snowfall. Rangers initiated a massive $35,000 search which included helicopters, avalanche dogs, winter climbers and skiers, but Massari was not found until June 18. During the search, rangers were involved in 15 avalanches, but no rescuers were hurt.

1991, August 23: The first Longs Peak Reunion of climbers, rangers, and other admirers of the peak was held coincidental with the 123rd anniversary of J. W. Powell's ascent. Events included an anniversary climb, historical displays, symposium of noted speakers, barbecue dinner, and art show.

1991, August 24: Howard and Huntoon were both struck unconscious by lightning near the Boulder Field solar privy. A passerby with a cellular telephone called for direct helicopter rescue from St. Anthony's Hospital in Denver and assisted with CPR efforts until the ship arrived about 20 minutes later. Both persons survived.

1991, October 12: Matt McClellan fell seventy feet from the Narrows to a small ledge, sustaining life-threatening head injuries. A team of volunteers and rangers led by Jim Detterline and Jim Richardson worked through the night in 80 mph winds to stabilize McClellan's injuries and transport him from the mountain.

1991, December: Seven climbing rangers traveled to the Andes Mountains of Venezuela to instruct 83 rescuers in state of the art techniques. Longs Peak continued its role in international rescue during the summer of 1992, when Williams Sarmiento of Merida, Venezuela, served as an exchange rescuer with the Longs Peak staff, participating in numerous missions.

1992, May 17: Jim Detterline assigned as first permanent Longs Peak Climbing Ranger.

1992, September 6: Paul Price broke his leg at the top of the Trough and was raised in a vertical litter-raising maneuver by the park rescue team to the summit, where a helicopter transported him directly to the hospital. This was the first successful litter-raising rescue operation on Longs Peak.

1993, May: The movie "Cliffhanger" opened in the Estes Park area. Starring Sylvester Stallone and Janine Turner, the movie featured a fanciful plot involving Longs Peak rangers in an attempt to deal with Denver Mint thieves who had crash landed an airplane on the peak.

1993, June: The Longs Peak Road was paved for the first time, in a joint project between Rocky Mountain National Park and Larimer County.

1993, August: Pope John Paul II visited the Longs Peak area and hiked from Camp St. Malo into the Cabin Creek drainage on Mt. Meeker.

1993, August 17: The Joker, put up in memory of Derek Hersey, was first established by Roger Briggs and Steve Levin (with two points of aid near the top), and first totally free climbed July 23, 1994, by Roger Briggs and Pat Adams.

1993, August 23: The 125th anniversary of J.W. Powell's ascent was celebrated with a Longs Peak Reunion, including a commemorative re-enactment climb of the Powell Route, barbecue, symposium of noted speakers, exhibit of Longs Peak art, major theme museum display at the Estes Park Historical Museum, guided hikes by famous climbers, and other special programs. Over 5,000 people attended.

1993, August: Helen Donahue, who had climbed the peak at age 6 (1927, with her father), climbed it again at age 72, assisted by her son, Mike Donahue.

1994, July 4: Cavrin Cowan of Estes Park, age 4 years, 357 days, set a record as the youngest person to climb Longs Peak under his own power.

1995, February 20: First one-day (25 hours 10 minutes parking lot to parking lot) ascent of the Diamond in winter, on D7 via the North Chimney by Gary Ryan and Gregory Crouch of Boulder.

1995, Summer: Late Spring snows that continued through the Fourth of July covered the high peaks, and made 1995 the first year that the Keyhole Route did not go non-technical or have a hiking season.

1995, July: Andrew Worm and partner made the first snowboard descent of the North Face of Longs Peak.

1995, Aug. 2: Tom Hornbein, at age 64, became the oldest person to climb the Diamond (via the Casual Route).

1996, Jan.: Topher Donahue and Craig Luebben climbed the Diamond in a one-day trail head to trail head winter speed record of 20 hrs., 40 min. Only 8 hrs. of that time was actually technical climbing. The remainder of the day was snow slogging on the trail.

1996, March: Kennan Harvey made the first one-day solo winter ascent of the Diamond and beat the previous winter Diamond speed record with a round trip time of only 17 hrs. trail head to trail head.

1996, July 14: Nate Dick lost control while glissading Lamb's Slide and slid 1000', impaling himself with his ice axe in the neck and right subclavian artery while attempting to self arrest. Witness Vladimir Farkash and other nearby climbers came to his rescue. Paramedic Mike Pratt was able to stop the bleeding and stabilize Dick for the evacuation down Mills Glacier by litter, across Chasm Lake by raft, and into a helicopter on the east shore of Chasm Lake.

1997, Jan. 5: The position of "climbing ranger" was removed from Longs Peak staff, making this the first year since 1936 that there were no climbing rangers stationed at Longs Peak.

1997, Oct. 11-14: Chris Sproul and David Sweedler got stormed in at the "open book" on top of Kiener's Route during a typical Autumn snow. A major search and rescue operation ensued in which the climbers were rescued but with serious frostbite to extremities.

1998, Aug. 1: Fran Bagenal fell 1000' while telemark skiing Lamb's Slide after three turns, fracturing her back in five places. Bystanders helped her to the bivouac caves. Rangers organized a rescue with the help of climbers, and raised Bagenal 1000' to a helispot and flight out on Mills Glacier in only 28 minutes, beating the incoming lightning storm by 5 minutes.

1998, Oct.: Isabella Bird Symposium was held in Estes Park to commemorate the 125th anniversary of her Longs Peak ascent.

2000, Jan. 1: Jim Detterline became the first person to climb Longs Peak in the new century, topping out solo up the North Face Route at 4:20 a.m.

2000: Archeologists Louise Elinoff and Daniel Bach discovered fragments of a stone knife, rock chips, and arrowheads at Jim's Grove, evidence of use of the former camping area by Early Archaic Native Americans 11,000 years ago.

2000, Feb. 7: Craig Dreher, who weighed 170 lbs. and was wearing a 70 lb. pack, was picked up off the ground by a wind estimated at 150 mph and thrown, resulting in a fractured leg at Boulderfield.

2000, July 12: Andy Haberkorn was fatally hit by lightning on the Diamond. The park rescue team raised him 600' up the Diamond and 300' up scree to the summit of Longs Peak in a two day effort that was interrupted by additional lightning storms.

2000, Oct. 1: A Longs Peak Rescue Symposium was held to celebrate the accomplishments of rescuers during the history of Longs Peak. Five persons were awarded the first Longs Peak Rescue Awards, including Dr. Hull Cook, Dr. Sam Luce, Walter Fricke, Billy Westbay, and John Gillett.

2000, Oct. 20: Jim Detterline set the record for the longest streak of consecutive monthly summits of Longs Peak, 2 years and 6 months (30 months). Jim had also climbed to the summit via East Face routes in every month of the year.

2001, Jan. 4: A hiker reported that both heavy-weight solar privies, which were cabled into nearby rocks, at Boulderfield had been blown over and destroyed by heavy winds. Two past attempts at measuring wind speeds with remote intrumentation on Longs Peak summit had failed when the apparatus blew apart after measuring windspeeds of 220mph.

2001, Aug. 25: Tommy Caldwell and Beth Rodden did the first ascent of the route "The Honeymoon Is Over" V 5.13c on the Diamond, which set a new standard as the peak's most difficult route.

2001, Aug. 19-26: A Longs Peak Reunion was held, hosted by Historical Preservations, Inc. The Longs Peak Rescue Award was given to climber Vlado Farkash and ranger Mike Pratt for their efforts on the 1996 Nate Dick rescue.

2002: USGS revised the elevation of Longs Peak from 14,255' to 14,259'.

2003, March 23: An avalanche destroyed Chasm Meadows Patrol Cabin. A storm from the previous week had deposited 8'-9' of fresh heavy snow atop a mostly compacted icy snowpack. With a shift in wind direction during early morning hours on March 23, the pack loosened and avalanched as one great mass from the Right Gully on Meeker north of the far end of the Saddle. It took only 45 seconds for the avalanche, traveling at 106 mph, to move 0.5 mile and knock down the stone cabin to its foundation and spread debris for an additional 0.5 mile to the east.

2003, May: George Bell Jr., Andy Moore, and Bernard Vachon made the first ski descent of Keplinger's Couloir, the original 1868 John Wesley Powell route, complete from the summit of Longs Peak into the Hunter's Creek drainage.

2003, June 23: A 13-year old girl fell on the snowfield above Peacock Pool, and was stopped from certain injury by ranger Ryan Schuster, who jumped onto the snowfield and caught the girl. Schuster was awarded the Longs Peak Rescue Award.

Interesting Events and Dates concerning Longs Peak

2003, Oct. 17: RMNP Wrangler Mike Schoedel and his pack train of 5 horses and mules got hit and were injured by a falling ice formation from the south face of Mt. Lady Washington as they were returning from the newly-constructed Chasm Meadows Patrol Cabin with tools and refuse.

2005, Jan. 20: Jamin Camp, a 28-year-old Aurora, Colorado, man became the first person to survive a 100 foot fall from the Narrows. Climbing guide John Bicknell of the Boulder Rock Club and Colorado Mountain School and his client, Denver Police officer Greg Jones, encountered the injured climber, who had dragged himself to the Chasm Junction area, a distance of four and one half miles. Bicknell called park staff with his cell phone at 7:30 p.m.; rescuers reached Jones and the victim at 11:51 p.m. A helicopter rescue was foiled by high winds, and the victim was carried out by a litter team, reaching the trailhead at 11:45 a.m., where an ambulance met the party and took the victim to Estes Park Medical Center.

North Face from Storm Peak

C Cable Route, CV Chasm View, D Dove, E Ev's Chimney, EF East Face, F False Keyhole or Transom, FK False Keyhole Ledge, KW Keyboard of the Winds, L Left or Direct Dovetail, M Mary's Ledges, MC Moss Chimney, N Northwest or Keyhole Ridge, R Right Dovetail, S Summit, Z Zumie's Chimney, ZT Zumie's Thumb

Those Who Have Climbed Longs Peak Most

1.	Shep Husted	350	12.	Alva Jones	120
2.	Enos Mills	305	13.	Paul Nesbit	116
3.	Bob Bradley	300	14.	Walter Tishma	113
4.	Otto Van Allman	255	15.	Walter Kiener	110
5.	Mike Donahue	250	16.	Dick Rutledge	106
6.	Jim Detterline	229	17.	Lester "Nick" Nickless	100
7.	Robert Collier	207	18.	Hull Cook	91
8.	Jack Moomaw	200	19.	Jim Disney	90
9.	Ernie Field	150	20.	Everett Long	89
10.	Carlyle Lamb	146	21.	Clerin Zumwalt	87
11.	George Greeley	121	22.	Paul Hauk	87

Life Spans of Some "Longs-Peakers"

Otto Van Allman 1920-1989	Derek Hersey 1956-1993
Paul Stettner 1906-1994	Ev Long 1911?-1995?
Clerin Zumwalt 1911-1996	Merrill Mattes 1911 -1996
Hull Cook 1911-2001	Joe Stettner 1901-1997
Billy Westbay 1954?-2000	Rod Willard 1960?-2002

Fast Climbing Records

1983, parking area to top, 1 hour 18 minutes 30 seconds, Mike Sullivan
July 26, 1979, top to parking area, 41 minutes 30 seconds, Chris Reveley
July 26, 1979, round trip from parking area, 2 hours 4 minutes 30 seconds, Chris Reveley

Altitudes Of Highest Peaks

World: Mount Everest, 29,035 feet	California: Mount Whitney, 14,495 feet
South America: Aconcagua, 22,834 feet	Colorado: Mount Elbert, 14,431 feet
North America: Mt. McKinley (Denali), 20,320	Washington: Mount Rainier, 14,410 feet
Canada: Mount Logan, 19,551 feet	Wyoming: Gannett Peak, 13,804 feet
Africa: Kilimanjaro, 19,341 feet	New Mexico: Wheeler Peak, 13,161 feet
Caucasus: El'brus, 18,510 feet	Montana: Granite Peak, 12,799 feet
Antarctica: Vinson Massif, 16,066 feet	Oregon: Mount Hood, 11,239 feet
New Guinea: Carstensz, 16,503 feet	Eastern U.S. (NC): Mount Mitchell, 6,684 feet
The Alps: Mont Blanc, 15,771 feet	New Hampshire: Mount Washington, 6,288 feet

Fatalities On or Near Longs Peak

1. Sept. 23, 1884, *Carrie J. Welton*, age 42, Waterbury, CT. Exhaustion and Exposure. Keyhole Formation.
2. Aug. 28, 1889, *Frank Stryker,* age 24, Tipton, IA. Accidental gunshot wound from carrying loaded pistol in his pocket, which fell out and discharged into his neck as he was trundelling rocks. Homestretch descent, with the same guide as Carrie J. Welton.
3. July 20, 1921, *Gregory Aubuchon*, age 18, Michigantown, IN. 1800' unroped fall, slid off snowfield between Cable Route and summit, over the Diamond to Mills Glacier.
4. Sept. 26, 1921, *H. F. Targett*, age 55, Los Angeles, CA. Unknown causes. Skull found 19 years later near Peacock Pool.
5. Aug. 1, 1922, *Jesse E. Kitts*, Greeley, CO. Lightning. Longs Peak summit.
6. Jan. 12, 1925, *Agnes W. Vaille*, age 31, Denver, CO. Minor leg injuries from a fall led to hypothermia. Base of North Face route.
7. Jan. 12, 1925, *Herbert Sortland*, age 22, Litchfield, ND. Broken hip probably from fall in snow—covered boulders led to hypothermia. Between east rim of Boulderfield and 300 yards west of Longs Peak Inn where body was found almost 2 months later (he was attempting to rescue Agnes Vaille and separated from the rescue party when he became too cold to continue).
8. July 23, 1926, *Forrest Keatring*, age 19, Denver, CO. 1000' unroped fall. Notch Couloir chimneys.
9. Aug. 18, 1929, *Charles Thiemeyer*, age 28, Denver, CO. 1500' Roped fall, belay failure. Notch Couloir Chimneys.
10. Sept. 18, 1931, *R. B. Key*, Lake, MS. Solo unroped fall. Mills Glacier.
11. July 18, 1932, *Robert F. Smith*, Michigan City, IN. Decapitated by falling rock. Base of Cables Route.
12. Aug. 29, 1932, *Gary Secor Jr.*, age 16, Longmont, CO. 150' unroped fall. False Keyhole shortcut.
13. Aug. 8, 1938, *John A. Fuller*, age 26, Ames, IA. 550' unroped tall on snow. Left Dove.
14. Aug. 7, 1939, *Gerald J. Clark*, age 37, Denver, CO. Hypothermia and head injury, new route near Field's Chimney (hung overnight and died as rescue party reached him the next day).
15. Sept. 1, 1946, *Charles Grant*, age 19, Chicago, IL. Fall, belay failure in attempting to stop his partner's fall of 60' (partner lived). Stettner's Ledges.
16. June 5, 1954, *Earl F. Harvey*, age 19, Gretna, VA. 500' fall, over Zumie's Chimney.
17. Aug. 15, 1956, *Rena Hoffman*, age 33, Chicago, IL. Lightning. Mills Moraine.
18. April 21, 1960, *David L. Jones*, age 18, Webster Groves, MO. 1000' fall after trying to hold on to rope with frostbitten hands. Homestretch.
19. April 21, 1960, *Prince D. Wilmon*, age 23, Fort Smith, AR. 400' fall after trying to hold on to rope with frostbitten hands. Homestretch, with David L. Jones.
20. Aug. 27, 1962, *Ken Murphy*, age 19, Kingfisher, OK. 100' fall. Off-route on descent of Keyhole Route and above the actual route.
21. Sept. 30, 1962, *James Scott O'Toole*, age 20, Pasadena, CA. Fall. Attempting to shortcut from the Keyhole Route over the ridge to Chasm View, and fell down the Left Dove.
22. Aug. 27, 1966, *C. Blake Hiester Jr.*, age 48, Denver, CO. 1200' unroped fall, from Notch Couloir chimneys over east face to bergschrund and 250' within Mills Glacier.
23. Sept. 11, 1971, *Rudolf Postweiler*, age 48, Boulder, CO. Heart attack. 3 miles up on East Longs Peak Trail.
24. Jan. 23, 1972, *Fred Stone*, age 20, Bellvue, CO. Probable broken leg led to hypothermia. Lower Roaring Fork. 25.
25. Jan. 23, 1972, *Joan Jardine*, age 21, Fort Collins, CO. Hypothermia. Lower Roaring Fork.
26. June 12, 1972, *Paul F. Russell*, age 24, Lincoln Park, MI. Unroped fall. East Chimney Route above the Narrows.
27. Aug. 12, 1972, *Gerald F. Murphy*, age 51, Westminister, CO. Heart attack. 1.5 Miles up on East Longs Peak Trail.
28. April 1, 1973, *Jay Van Stavern*, age 19, Boulder, CO. 1800' unroped fall, slid off snowfield between Cable Route and summit, over the Diamond to Mills Glacier (left ice axe stuck at top of Diamond).

29. Aug. 20, 1973, *Joseph Holub*, age 22, Huntsville, AL. 200' fall. Ships Prow.

30. Aug. 24, 1975, **William Gizzie**, Littleton, CO. Heart attack or hypothermia. Chasm Meadow.

31. June 1, 1977, *Michael G. Neri*, age 21, Estes Park, CO. Slipped on wet vegetation and took 600' unroped fall with 80 lb. pack from Broadway Ledge down to Mills Glacier.

32. Sept. 16, 1978, *Harvey Schneider,* age 22, Boulder, CO. Unroped fall. Lambs Slide.

33. Sept. 1, 1979, *Dr. Edward Sujansky*, age 43, Denver, CO. Heart attack. Keyhole Formation after successful ascent.

34. Oct. 6, 1979, *Charles Nesbit*, (no relation to the author) age 36, Golden, CO. 600' unroped sliding fall. Lamb's Slide.

35. Nov. 14, 1979, *Kris Gedney,* age 22, Boulder, CO. Suicide by ingestion of antifreeze and fall. Narrows.

36. June 26, 1980, *Robert Slyer*, age 16, Cedar Rapids, IA. Fall. Homestretch.

37. Jan. 10, 1981, *Robert Elliot,* age 26, Eldorado Springs, CO. 90' belayed fall due to intermediate anchor failure resulted in fatal spinal injuries. Broadway Ledge above North Chimney.

38. Dec. 14, 1981, *James P. Duffy III*, age 24, Marshall, CO. Hypothermia. Descent to the Ledges in winter conditions after ascent of East Face, with same partner as Robert Elliot.

39. Sept. 12, 1986, *Dr. Lawrence N. Farrell*, age 33, Fort Collins, CO. Unroped fall, traverse between Homestretch and Keplinger's Couloir.

40. Aug. 10, 1988, *Roger Kevin Hardwick*, age 30, Morrison, CO. 900' unroped sliding fall. Lamb's Slide.

41. July 21, 1989, *Evan R. Corbett*, age 20, Boulder, CO. Suicide by ingestion of 85 sleeping pills and 500' jump from summit into Trough.

42. Aug. 25, 1989, *Albert N. Fincham*, age 52, Streator, IL. Heart attack. 4 miles up on East Longs Peak Trail.

43. July 29, 1990, *Timothy M. Fromalt*, age 27, Longmont, CO. Stopped falling girlfriend but slipped on wet rock and fell 60'. Homestretch.

44. April 22, 1991, *Joe Massari*, age 45, Boulder, CO. 1500' unroped fall. Kiener's Route in high avalanche conditions.

45. Feb. 3, 1993, *Carl Siegel*, age 30, Boulder, CO. 500' unroped fall. Descending Cables Route after successful winter Diamond ascent.

46. Sept. 14, 1993, *Kelly Thomas*, age 27, Thornton, CO. Hypothermia. Stormed off unsuccessful attempt of Kiener's Route and died on north shore of Chasm Lake.

47. Aug. 25, 1995, *Jun Kamimura*, age 33, Japan. 400' unroped fall. Ledges in technical conditions.

48. Sept. 9, 1997, *Timothy M. Maron*, age 26, Denver, CO. 220' unroped fall. Ascending or descending the Loft enroute to/from Longs Peak.

49. Aug.3, 1999, *Raymond R. Decker*, age 75, Baton Rouge, LA. Slip on black ice and 150' unroped fall. Narrows.

50. Aug. 4, 1999, *James Page*, age 56, Clinton, NY. 90' unroped fall. Gorrell's Traverse.

51. Aug. 14, 1999, *Gregory J. Koczanski*, age 42, Vienna, VA. 450' unroped fall. Ledges.

52. March 4, 2000, *Colby Sharp*, age 28, Boulder, CO. 300' unroped fall on loose snow. Ascending the Loft enroute to Longs Peak.

53. July 6, 2000, *Cameron Tague,* age 32, Boulder, CO. 799' unroped fall, base of Yellow Wall down Fields' Chimney to Mills Glacier.

54. July 12, 2000, *Andy Haberkorn*, age 28, Boulder, CO. Lightning. Casual Route on the Diamond.

55. September 4, 2004, *Sudheer Averineni*, age 26, Fort Collins, CO and India. Exposure. Summit after ascent of Keyhole Route.

Bibliography

Alberts, Edwin C., *Rocky Mountain National Park, Colorado*. U.S. Dept. of Interior. Government Printing Office. 1954.

American Alpine Journal, The and *Accidents in North American Mountaineering*. Both published by the American Alpine Club, 710 Tenth St., Suite 100, Golden, CO 80401

Arps, Louis Ward and Kingery, Elinor Eppich, *High Country Names*, Colorado Mountain Club, 710 Tenth St., Golden, CO 80401, 1966

Bird, Isabella L., *A Lady's Life in the Rocky Mountains*. Republished as a paperback by Oklahoma Press, 1960.

Briggs, Roger, "Longs Peak Face Climbs," *Rock and Ice Magazine*, March-April, 1986.

Cargo, David and Chisholm, Richard, *Rocky Mountain National Park - Outdoorsman's Guide*, 1966, David Cargo, 1974 San Ildefonso, Santa Fe, N.M. 87501.

Carothers, J. E, *Estes Park, Past and Present*, University of Denver Press, 1951.

Chapin, Frederick H. *Mountaineering In Colorado*, The Appalachian Mountain Club, 1889. Reprinted by the University of Nebraska Press, 1987.

Colorado Mountain Club and Robert M. Ormes, *Guide to the Colorado Mountains*, 9th Edition revised by Randy Jacobs. Distributed by Cordillera Press, Evergreen, 1992.

Dannen, Kent and Donna, *Rocky Mountain National Park Hiking Trails*, 7th edition, Globe Pequot, Chester, Conn., 1989.

Dickinson, Anna. *A Ragged Register*, Harper Bros., 1879.

Donahue, Helen Hannen, et al, *Three Sisters Remember Longs Peak in 1927*, Indiana Camp Supply, Inc., Loveland, 1993.

Donahue, Mike, *The Longs Peak Experience*, Indiana Camp Supply, Inc., Loveland, 1992.

Dunning, Harold M., *Over Hill and Vale*. Vols. I, 1956, and II, 1962, Harold M. Dunning, 126 South Lincoln, Loveland, CO. 80536.

Dunning, Harold M., *The History of Estes Park*, excerpts from the above. Same publisher and address as above. Third printing, 1966.

Dunning, Harold M. *Facts About Longs Peak*, Same publisher and address as above. First printing, 1970.

DuMais, Richard. *The High Peaks*, High Peak Books, Boulder, CO., 1981.

Eberhart, Perry and Philip Schmuck, *The Fourteeners, Colorado's Great Mountains*, The Swallow Press, Inc., 1139 So. Wabash Avenue, Chicago, IlL 60605. First printing, 1970.

Estes Park Trail-Gazette, Estes Park, CO. Local twice weekly newspaper.

Fricke, Walter W. Jr., *A Climber's Guide to the Rocky Mountain National Park Area*, Published by Walter Fricke, 1720 So. Marshall Road, Boulder, Co. 80303. First printing, 1971.

Gillett, Bernard, *Rocky Mountain National Park: The Climber's Guide*, Earthbound Sports Inc., P.O. Box 3312, Chapel Hill, NC 27515, 1993.

Gorby, John D., *The Stettner Way: the Life and Climbs of Joe and Paul Stettner*, Colorado Mountain Club Press, 2003

Harlin, John III, *The Climber's Guide to North America: Rocky Mountain Rock Climbs*, Chockstone Press, Evergreen, CO., 1985.

Hart, John L. Jerome, *Fourteen Thousand Feet*. Published by the Colorado Mountain Club, Denver, 1925. A History of the names and early ascents of the High Colorado Peaks.

Hawthorne, Hildegard and Esther B. Mills, *Enos Mills of the Rockies* 1935.

Hayden, Dr. F. V. *Annual Reports,* 1873, U.S. Geological Survey.

Hewes, Charles Edwin, *Songs of the Rockies*, Revised 1938. Published by the author.

Kimball, Scott, *Lumpy Ridge - Estes Park Rock Climbs*, Chockstone Press, Evergreen, CO. 1986.

Lamb, the Rev. E. J., *Memories of the Past and Thoughts of the Future* - autobiography, United Brethren Publishing House, 1906.

Lee, Willis T., *The Geologic Story of the Rocky Mountain National Park, Colorado*. Published by the National Park Service, 1917.

Long, John, *How to Rock Climb.* Globe Pequot Press, Guilford, CT., 2002.

MacDonald, Dougald. *Longs Peak: The Story of Colorado's Favorite Fourteener.* Westcliffe Publishers, Evergreen, CO. 2004

Mills, Enos A., *The Story of Estes Park* 1911. Republished in 1959 and 1963 as *Early Estes Park* by the late Esther B. Mills (Mrs. Enos A. Mills) and with a foreword by her. Among several books by Mr. Mills, the following are noteworthy or contain material about Longs Peak: *Wild Life on the Rockies*, 1909, *Rocky Mountain Wonderland*, 1915, Houghton Mifflin Co., *Adventures of a Nature Guide*, 1920, and *The Rocky Mountain National Park*, 1924, Doubleday Page and Co. Some available from Enos Mills Cabin, 6760 Highway 7, Estes Park, CO 80517-6404 http://home.earthlink.net/~enosmillscbn/

Moomaw, Jack C., *Recollections of a Rocky Mountain Ranger,* YMCA of the Rockies, Estes Park, 1994 (new edition, with emendations, of the 1963 volume).

Musselman, Lloyd K., *Rocky Mountain National Park - Its First Fifty Years - 1915-1965*, Rocky Mountain Nature Association (in cooperation with the National Park Service), Estes Park, CO., 1965.

Off Belay Magazine, 12416 169th S.E., Renton, Wash. 98055.

Pickering, James H., *This Blue Hollow: Estes Park, the Early Years, 1859-1915,* University Press of Colorado, Boulder, 1999

Roach, Gerry, *Rocky Mountain National Park: Classic Hikes and Climbs*, Fulcrum Press, Golden, CO., 1989.

Robertson, Janet, *The Magnificent Mountain Women*, University of Nebraska Press, Lincoln, 1990.

Robinson, Peter, *Technical Rock Climbers' Guide to the East Face of Longs Peak*, 1966. Unpublished. Typewritten copy at Longs Peak Ranger Station.

Rossiter, Richard, *An Interim Rock Climbing Guide to Rocky Mountain National Park*, Chockstone Press Inc., P.O. Box 3505, Evergreen, CO 80439, 1992

Toll, Oliver W., *Arapahoe Names and Trails*, Oliver Toll, Tolland, CO., 1963.

Toll, Roger W., *Mountaineering in Rocky Mountain National Park*, published by the National Park Service, 1921.

Trail and Timberline, published monthly by the Colorado Mountain Club, 710 Tenth Street, Suite 100, Golden CO 80401, www.cmc.org, has contained several articles pertaining to Longs Peak. January 1968 was a Longs Peak issue.

Trimble, Stephen, *Longs Peak: A Rocky Mountain Chronicle,* Rocky Mountain Nature Association, Estes Park, CO., 1983.

Wadman, Clay, *Longs Peak and the Diamond Climbers Topo Guide to the East Face of Longs Peak*, Diamond Productions, 2525 Arapahoe Ave., Suite E4-336, Boulder, CO 80302, 1994.

West Side of Longs Peak from Chiefs Head

F False Keyhole, G Gorrell's Traverse, H Homestretch, K To Keyhole, KW Keyboard of the Winds, L Loft or Saddle, M Mt. Meeker, N Narrows, P Pagoda Peak, PS Palisades, S Shelf or Ledges, SW Southwest Ridge, T Trough, VW Van Diver's West Wall, W West Wall, WC West Couloir *(arrow indicates it goes behind ridge).* Bruns and Fourth of July routes not located.

Photo by — John McDowell

The Hannen Clan Ascents of Longs Peak — 394 Total

Dr. F. S. Hannen — 10
Minnie M. Hannen — 4

| Francis R. Hannen — 30
Vivian J. Hannen — 5 | Marjie Hannen Bickel — 14
George Bickel — 6 | Irene St. John — 7
Al St. John — 2 |

Vicki Hannen — 1
Bruce Hannen — 3

Gary Bickel — 18
Mark Bickel — 1

Danny St. John — 7

Casey Hannen — 2
Heidi Hannen — 1

Helen (Hannen) Donahue — 29
Warren Donahue — 10

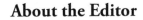

Pat Donahue — 2
Mike Donahue — 200

The family table shown here is given as an example of the appeal climbing Longs Peak has for people and for some families.
Dr. and Mrs. Hannen made a total of 14 climbs. Through 1995, their descendents had accounted for 380 additional climbs and there have been more since.

Topher Donahue — 30
Nem Donahue — 4
Tobias Donahue — 2

Brian Donahue — 4
Tobin Donahue — 1
Kerry Donahue — 1

Helen Hannen, age 6 at the summit in August, 1927 on the first of 29 climbs

About the Editor

Dr. Stan Adamson grew up in Los Angeles and graduated from the Film School at UCLA in 1970. Since 1987, he has been the Pastor of St. Andrew Presbyterian Church in Boulder, Colorado. He holds a Doctor of Ministry degree from McCormick Theological Seminary in Chicago.

Stan developed his love of hiking as a small child, and then he and his wife taught their four sons to hike, backpack and climb, primarily in Rocky Mountain National Park for the past thirty years.

He edited the 9th and 10th editions of *Paul Nesbit's Longs Peak* at the invitation of Mills Publishing in Halstead, Kansas. For several years in the early 1990s, he taught the Longs Peak Adventure class for the Boulder Valley Schools Community Schools program. He has served as a co-host for several historical symposia connected with the Longs Peak reunions, which gave him the privilege of meeting many of the climbers mentioned in this book.